AN ILLUSTRATED GUIDE TO
AIRCRAFT
MARKINGS

PRENTICE HALL PRESS
New York   London   Toronto   Sydney   Tokyo

AN ILLUSTRATED GUIDE TO

AIRCRAFT MARKINGS

Barry C. Wheeler

A Salamander Book

An Arco Aviation Book

Published by Prentice Hall Press
A Division of Simon & Schuster, Inc.
Gulf + Western Building
One Gulf + Western Plaza
New York, NY 10023

This book may not be sold outside the
United States of America and Canada.

PRENTICE HALL PRESS is a
trademark of Simon & Schuster, Inc.

10 9 8 7 6 5 4 3 2

**Library of Congress
Cataloging-in-Publication Data**

Wheeler, Barry C.
  An illustrated guide to aircraft markings.

  ''An Arco aviation book.''
  1. Airplanes, Military — Identification marks.
2. Airplanes, Military — Camouflage. I. Title.
UG1240.W48 1986   358.4'183   86-12334
ISBN 0-13-451105-0

Credits

Author: Barry C. Wheeler is a defence
journalist. Formerly on the staff of *Flight
International*, he is currently Editor of the
Joint Services Recognition Journal.

Editor: Bernard Fitzsimons
Art Editor: Mark Holt
Designed by Stonecastle Graphics

Camouflage artwork: Terry Hadler
Insignia artwork: ©Pilot Press Ltd.
Other artwork: James Goulding,
Mike Keep, Mark Franklin, Kai Choi

Typeset: The Old Mill, London
Printed in Belgium by Proost
International Book Production
Turnhout

All correspondence concerning
the content of this book
should be addressed to
Salamander Books Ltd.
52 Bedford Row
London WC1R 4LR
United Kingdom

Acknowledgements

In compiling this book, the author would like to acknowledge the kind assistance of many people, in particular Dennis Baldry, Philip Barley, Robert F. Dorr, Richard Gardner, Dave Howley, Mike Stroud and Dick Ward. The publishers are also grateful to all those who supplied photographs used in this book.

Contents

Introduction

'Solve the problem of canopy glint and you could earn a fortune' observered a British camouflage expert wryly. No matter how effective aircraft camouflage is, the merest reflection from a cockpit canopy can compromise its concealment and give away the machine's position possibly to an enemy pilot and with likely fatal results.

For centuries, colour and insignia have been associated with military forces. In ancient times Roman legions raised their own distinguishing standard to indicate their position, while in China armies divided into units, each carrying a different plain-coloured flag, and the advent of armour in the Middle Ages and the widespread use of helmets that hid the faces of the wearers led to the adoption of brightly-coloured surcoats and shields for identification. British Army regiments took up the use of the standard known as the Colours and these were symbolic of the very spirit of the regiment being carried into battle in the centre of the line, always closely guarded; where they stopped, there the regiment stood, and if necessary the last man would defend the Colours to the death. To lose the Colours was the ultimate disgrace.

The arrival of the aeroplane early in this century called for some kind of distinguishing mark to indicate its operator and nationality. Although the flags were flown from airships, it was not aerodynamically practical to display them from aircraft, so the national emblem was painted on the wings, tails and/or fuselages of early machines. Military markings for aircraft were agreed under the Hague Convention 1907, while the registration of civilian aircraft was instituted internationally in 1919 by the Paris Air Convention.

Current national insignia generally relate to national flags and designs vary considerably. Colours also correspond in most cases to the national emblem, though there is a growing trend to reduce or eliminate altogether brightness in combat aircraft

markings. In their place pastel shades are being applied and in some cases only outlines of the original markings are carried. A state of tension between countries or even open conflict will result in national insignia being reduced in size or possibly removed completely, which is fine if you have air superiority or an effective IFF (identification friend or foe) system: if not, mis-identification can lead to aircraft being shot down by friendly forces.

All markings carried by modern combat aircraft have a role to play, from the smallest 'no step' which prevents personnel unfamiliar with the machine from damaging parts of the airframe, to large tail codes which identify units and sometimes bases. A diminishing number of markings are now applied to Western front-line machines, which reduces costs but is a cause of frustration to the large number of enthusiasts world-wide who follow this subject. In fact they have not been served too

Above: Reflection bouncing off the engine intakes and canopy of a US Navy F-14A Tomcat prior to the application of matt paint.

Below: Official specification for RAF roundels. The diameter (D) varies according to the size of the aircraft.

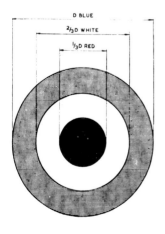

ROUNDELS—STANDARD

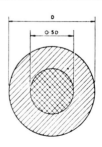

ROUNDEL BLUE
BS.381C/110

POST OFFICE RED
BS.381C/538

KEY

ROUNDELS—CAMOUFLAGED AIRCRAFT

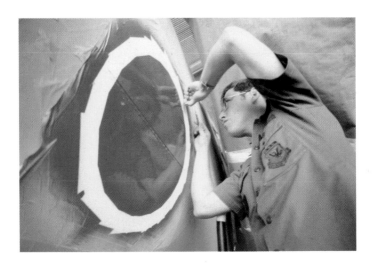

Above: One way of doing it. Tech Sgt Ronald Breeman removes the masking on a Japanese F-15 following the application of the national marking. While the majority of large insignia are sprayed on, an increasing number are applied as self-adhesive transfers.

Below: One of many official US schemes applied to F-5Es.

Right: During trials to determine the most effective tactics to be used by USAF A-10A Thunderbolts, a series of camouflage schemes were evaluated by the 57th TTW in November 1977. This mottled scheme was applied to every part of the aircraft and was changed from day to day to match weather and terrain conditions.

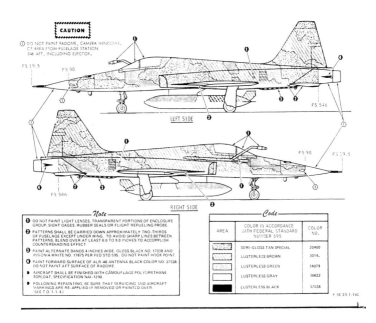

well in recent years. Not only have markings faded, but the aircraft that carry them have gone to ground — or, more correctly, the front-line NATO force has been positioned in hardened aircraft shelters (HAS) throughout Western Europe, to lessen the chances of destruction from a surprise attack. Consequently, a look across a military airfield today will generally produce a scene barren of combat aircraft, but covered with small camouflaged hangarettes in which the warplanes sit armed and ready. It should be mentioned that the Eastern Bloc also have adopted this idea, although the freedom to walk up to the fence of a Warsaw Pact base is denied to all but the foolhardy.

Hand in hand with the general toning down of markings is the use of dull but practical camouflage colours: the Vietnam war put paid to the polished metal finishes of the 1950s and 1960s and drab disruptive schemes took over. Initially greens and browns dominated the scene, but in recent years fighters have donned greys in what has become

known as counter-shading of very similar colours. Whereas the use of grey can be traced back to its application by the Luftwaffe during World War II, the new colours are subtle and amazingly effective. Evolved by a process of experimentation, the latest schemes can be considered the very best in low-visibility camouflage. However, they must also be able to withstand the constant attention of maintenance crews and be weather resistant. The paint manufacturers are constantly striving for better products and to meet new requirements from the air forces such as radar-absorbent paint. For aircraft not designed for 'stealth'

operations, the next best thing is to cover them with a material which will absorb the radar signals and reduce their signature and therefore their liability to detection.

This book considers only the combat aircraft in current service with the world's air forces, although where applicable other types are noted in the context of front-line use. Throughout the text, references to British colours are related to the British Standard series BS381C and BS4800 followed by the individual number. The equivalent American series are known as Federal Standard No 595a Colours. Each five-figure reference number for the actual col-

our has an initial digit which indicates whether it is (1) glossy, (2) semi-gloss or (3) lustreless (or matt). The second digit indicates the selected colour classification group, while the last three figures indicate the approximate order of increasing (diffuse) reflectance and are assigned non-consecutively to leave gaps for future additions.

Model-makers should find these references useful, although no attempt has been made to match them to the various specialized model paint ranges as this book is not intended as a modelling guide. Nothing remains static for very long and colour schemes and markings

Above: Don't be fooled by the bright colours carried by modern service aerobatic team aircraft. Most have a war role, as shown by this Italian Air Force MB.339PAN of the *Frecce Tricolori*, equipped with pod-mounted cannon and iron bombs. Fifteen have been delivered to the team.

constantly change, sometimes imperceptibly and at others quite markedly. The name of the game is to improve aircrew and aircraft survivability and, with this in mind, the subject of colours and insignia will always hold a fascination.

National Insignia

Afghanistan

The present Afghan Republican Air Force insignia was adopted following the Soviet intervention of December 1979, replacing a triangular marking comprising the traditional Mohammedan colours of red, green and black in segmented form. In the new insignia, the central star represents

Albania

Due to the secretive nature of the country's Communist regime, photographs of combat aircraft operated by the Albanian People's Army Air Force are almost non-existent, and those that have been released show few points of interest regarding markings. The force's

Algeria

This former French colony has an air arm equipped largely with aircraft of Soviet origin, particularly in the front-line combat squadrons. Known as Al Quwwat Aljawwiya Aljza'eriiya, the Algerian Air Force has about 20 MiG-25 'Foxbat' interceptor and reconnaissance aircraft supported by 70 MiG-21 'Fishbed's, while ground-attack equipment includes MiG-23 'Flogger's and Su-7 and Su-20 'Fitter's, plus some ageing MiG-17 'Fresco's. These and other aircraft in service carry the national marking, formed by the colours of Islam, on wings and fuselage. A flash is also normally applied on the fin, and three-digit numbers, often in arabic form, are painted on the nose to indicate the individual aircraft in the squadron. Transport and other types have a call-sign prefixed 7T, examples being 7T-WFT, a Potez Magister, and 7T-WHY, applied to one of 16 Lockheed C-130 Hercules bought by the Air Force.

the current socialist government. Most ARAF combat aircraft (MiG-21s, MiG-23s and Su-17s) carry the symbol on the fins and wings, and have a three-digit identification number each side of the nose. Early MiG-17s were given a two-number code on the nose, but these elderly aircraft have now been withdrawn from front-line service. Afghan attack helicopters (Mi-24 'Hind-D's and Mi-8 'Hip-F's) also carry a three-number code and the national insignia on each side of the tail boom as well as on the underside of the fuselage.

Chinese Shenyang F-6 (MiG-19) and F-7 (MiG-21) fighters carry the national markings on wings and fuselage and have an identification number on the nose — three digits in the case of the F-6s (eg 3-34) and four on the F-7s (eg 0208). It is doubtful if any form of regimental insignia is carried although this cannot be confirmed. Transport aircraft, such as the small number of Il-14s in service, display a red and black flag on the rudder together with a small black code derived from the constructor's number identifying the individual machine.

Angola

As indicated by the insignia, Angola has a Marxist government; the country began receiving aid from the Soviet Union in 1976 following independence from Portugal. In addition to the national markings, the MiG-21s, MiG-23s and Su-22s of the Força Aérea Popular de Angola (Angolan People's Air Force) are given a two-digit number prefixed by the letter C indicating Caça (fighter). Attack helicopters are used increasingly by FAPA against UNITA guerrillas in the southeast of the country, the present fleet of Mi-24/25 'Hind's and Mi-8 'Hip's carrying two figures prefixed by the letter H. Second-line types are given a three-letter civilian registration prefixed by the national code D2.

Above: Algeria is one of a number of countries that operate military aircraft with civil registrations: Lockheed C-130H Hercules carries 7T WHY on the fin and above the starboard wing.

Argentina

Air Force

Navy

The blue and white insignia of the Fuerza Aérea Argentina became familiar to British servicemen during the 1982 Falklands War, when Argentina committed her air force to the first major conflict of its existence. The FAA, established as a separate arm in 1945, operated a mixed force of Mirage Vs, Israeli Daggers and A-4 Skyhawks on long-range attack sorties against British targets and gained respect from both sides for the way missions were pressed home against barrages of missiles and gunfire. In the absence of a formal cessation of hostilities, Argentina remained technically at war with Britain.

The aircraft roundel has the same colours as the national ensign and on FAA types is carried above and below the wings and on the rear fuselage. The fin flash is an exact miniature of the national flag and includes the 'Sun of May' marking in the centre commemorating the country's independence in 1810. Three-number codes indicate the individual aircraft, each prefixed by a role letter: C for Caza (fighter), B for Bombardeo (bomber), A for Ataque (attack), T for Transporte or H for helicopters. For identification at dispersal, the aircraft number is normally repeated on the nosewheel door. Combat types also carry FUERZA AEREA ARGENTINA in black along the nose.

Unit *esprit de corps* is encouraged by the large badges applied on the fins of the Mirages and Daggers, and on the noses of the Skyhawks. During the Falklands conflict yellow panels were applied to wings, fuselages and tails in an effort to reduce the risk of being fired at by friendly ground forces. These were subsequently removed.

Argentina's naval air arm (Comando de Aviación Naval Argentina) operates Super Etendards and A-4 Skyhawks from both shore bases and the country's sole aircraft carrier, *Veinticinco de Mayo*. An anchor

motif replaces the roundel and is carried above and below the wings, usually in white against dark camouflage and black on light backgrounds. ARMADA is painted on the rear fuselage, while the tail flash is applied across the full width of the rudder and the fin has a blue tip. Naval aircraft carry a prominent unit designator on the fuselage or fin, consisting of the Escuadra (wing) number, a role letter and a three-digit number combining the Escuadrilla (squadron) to which the aircraft is assigned with the number of the individual machine. Thus, Super Etendard 3-A-204, flown by 3ª Escuadra Aeronaval in the *A*ttack role, is operated by 2ª Escuadrilla Aeronaval de Caza y Ataque and is the *fourth* machine in the unit.

Army-operated aircraft and helicopters normally carry a three-digit number prefixed by AE for Aviación del Ejército. An example is AE-413, a Bell UH-1H captured by British forces in the Falklands and now in the UK. Unit badges are painted on the crew entry doors and the word EJERCITO is carried on the tail boom.

Below: Three of the Argentine Navy's Super Etendard carrier-based attack aircraft that flew with such dramatic results in the 1982 Falklands War. Note the anchor sign on both wings.

Australia

The present Australian roundel incorporating a kangaroo was adopted after the Second World War and replaced the previous style, which was identical to that used on RAF aircraft. However, the fin flash used on Royal Australian Air Force and Australian Army machines remains unchanged and is always applied red leading. The roundel is applied to both sides of the forward fuselage of F-111s, Mirage IIIs and F-18 Hornets, and to the underside of the wings on the Mirages. 'Miniature' markings are carried on the top of the port wing and on the black-painted underside of the starboard wing of F-111s, the kangaroo always facing forward with its legs toward the wingtip. These swing-wing bombers also carry a small Australian flag at the top of the fin and a unit badge prominently displayed in the form of a yellow flash for 1 Sqn and a blue flash for 6 Sqn. Unit markings are also painted on the Mirages and Hornets as well as on the transport and support aircraft.

The present system of identifying types used by the RAAF, Royal Australian Navy and Australian Army Aviation Corps involves the use of a letter A and a suffix number. The present A-series began in 1961 and followed two previous series, the first of which originated during World War I. The identification number is usually applied on both sides of the rear fuselage between the tailplane and the national insignia, although some aircraft and helicopters carry it on the fin and tailboom respectively.

Army-operated aircraft fall within the RAAF numbering system, but RAN helicopters carry an N prefix followed by the number. The accompanying list (see overleaf) is correct up to January 1986. ▶

RAAF/AAC aircraft type numbers

A2-	Bell UH-1H Iroquois	US-built, used by RAAF for Army support
A3-	Mirage IIIO/IIIDO	Australian-assembled, to be replaced by F-18 Hornet
A4-	DHC-4 Caribou	RAAF tactical transport
A7-	MB.326H	Standard RAAF jet trainer
A8-	F-111C/RF-111C	Main RAAF low-level attack and reconnaissance aircraft
A9-	P-3C Orion	ASW and maritime patrol aircraft
A10-	HS.748	RAAF navigation and VIP aircraft
A11-	Dassault Falcon 20	Three VIP aircraft
A12-	BAC One-Eleven Srs 217	Two VIP aircraft
A14-	PC-6 Turbo-Porter	Army transport and liaison
A15-	CH-47C Chinook	RAAF medium-lift helicopter
A17-	Bell 206B-1	Australian-built for Army use
A18-	GAF N22M Nomad	Army transport designed and built in Australia
A19-	CT-4A Airtrainer	RAAF basic pilot trainer
A20-	Boeing 707-338C	Four tanker conversions for use with F-18s
A21-	F/A-18 Hornet	Australian-assembled, to replace Mirages
A22-	AS.350 Squirrel	Trainer and SAR helicopter
A97-	C-130E/H Hercules	Standard RAAF transport (numbered in previous A-series)

Royal Australian Navy aircraft type numbers

N7-	Wessex HAS.31	Ship-based ASW and SAR
N9-	Bell UH-1B/C Iroquois	Being replaced by Squirrels on utility duties and SAR
N15-	HS.748	Two ECM aircraft
N16-	Sea King Mk 50/50A	Westland-built, operated on ASW duties
N17-	Bell 206B-1	Australian-built, three operated

Austria

The red and white national marking was first adopted by the Austrian Air Force in April 1936 and re-adopted by the reconstituted air arm in 1955. The Österreichische Luftstreitkräfte (Austrian Air Force) operates only one combat type, the Saab 105Ö. These aircraft are unpainted and carry the national insignia on the forward fuselage and on both upper and lower wings, and each carries a single letter on the fin in one of four Staffel (squadron) colours, yellow, green, red and blue. Saab Drakens will begin to replace the 105s in 1987.

Other types in Austrian service are given a number/letter prefix and a two-letter individual code, an example being 3C-JF, an Italian-built AB.206A JetRanger. The current prefix list is: 3C- AB.206A/Bell OH-58B; 3E- Alouette III; 3F-Saab 91D Safir; 3G- PC-6 Turbo-Porter; 3H-PC-7 Turbo-Trainer; 5D- AB.212; 5S- Short Skyvan. Most of these machines are painted dark green over the top surfaces with the codes applied in black, often split by the national insignia.

Bangladesh

Formerly East Pakistan, Bangladesh became an independent state in December 1971 and established a defensive air arm as part of the new country's Defence Forces. Initially equipped with a dozen MiG-21s supplied by the Soviet Union, the Bangladesh Air Force subsequently received more than 30 Shenyang F-6s (MiG-19s) from China and grounded the -21s because of a lack of spares. The F-6s are camouflaged and carry the national insignia on the wings and fuselage, plus a three-digit number of which 628 and 631 are examples. The green and red colours represent the fertility of the land and the blood shed in the struggle for independence.

Belgium

Air Force

Navy

A member of NATO, Belgium has her military flying units attached to the Alliance's 2nd Allied Tactical Air Force along with British, Dutch and West German elements. The Force Aérienne Belge or Belgische Luchtmacht, depending on whether your language is French or Flemish, groups all flying and non-flying combat units — four F-16 and four Mirage 5 escadrilles (squadrons), plus transport and training units — under Tactical Air Command.

The Belgian flag dates back to 1830 when the country gained its independence from the Netherlands, and most FAB combat aircraft carry a representation of this insignia on their fins, black leading on both sides. Roundels, usually thinly outlined in medium blue against a camouflaged background, are applied only on the wings of the F-16s and Mirages, their size having diminished in recent years in accordance with NATO's toned-down markings requirements. Rescue, warning and maintenance stencilling is applied in accordance with NATO standards, the F-16s retaining their factory grey colours together with the markings applied prior to delivery.

The FAB has a number of squadrons with histories going back to World War I and the proud tradi- ▶

F-16 squadron badges

1 Wing	349 Sqn 'Goedendag' or crossed clubs in a circle
	350 Sqn 'Ambiorix' (Viking head)
10 Wing	23 Sqn Red Devil
	31 Sqn Tiger badge

Mirage 5 squadron badges

2 Wing	2 Sqn red/yellow Comet
3 Wing	1 Sqn Thistle insignia, often in white
	8 Sqn Paper Horse or Cocotte usually in white on a blue background
42 Sqn	Mephisto or winged figure in red within a circle

tions of these units is exemplified by the badges carried on today's aircraft, usually applied to both sides of the aircraft's fin.

All FAB aircraft are assigned a serial number, usually located on the tail and consisting of a two-letter prefix indicating the type of aircraft followed by a sequential number. Current examples are shown in the accompanying table.

The Belgian Army operates Alouette IIs and B-N Islanders and employs the standard national insignia marking. Three Alouette IIIs form a Naval Flight, each machine carrying the roundel with a superimposed anchor marking in white. A call-sign is also carried (OT-ZPA, -ZPB and -ZPC), this being located on the main cabin door sill in white.

Belgian AF serial numbers

Mirage 5BA	BA 01 to BA 63
Mirage 5BD	BD 01 to BD 16
Mirage 5BR	BR 01 to BR 27
F-16A	FA 01 to FA 94
F-16B	FB 01 to FB 20
Alpha Jet	AT 01 to AT 33
C-130H Hercules	CH 01 to CH 12
HS.748	CS 01 to CS 03
SA-26T Merlin IIA	CF 01 to CF 06
SF.260MB	ST 01 to ST 36
CM.170R Magister	MT 01 to MT 50
Sea King Mk 48	RS 01 to RS 05

Benin

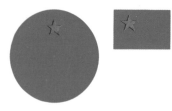

Formerly called Dahomey, the small former French colony of Benin currently has no combat aircraft within the Forces Armées Populaires du Benin, operating instead a modest collection of transport and liaison types. Aircraft in use include some Douglas C-47s, Antonov An-26s and an F.27-600. As well as the national insignia, aircraft carry registrations such as TY-ACC, which is applied to a C-47.

Bolivia

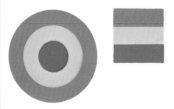

A handful of ex-Venezuelan F-86F Sabres have formed the fighter backbone of the Fuerza Aérea Boli-

Brazil

The largest air arm in South America, the Força Aérea Brasileira has a balanced combat inventory on which the only operational constraint is a tight financial budget. This has meant that the Mirage IIIs and F-5Es will not be replaced by more modern types such as the F-16 and Mirage 50, although toward the end of the 1980s the FAB will begin to receive the first of an anticipated 79 AMX light attack aircraft which are being built jointly by Embraer in Brazil and Aeritalia in Italy.

The national star insignia is formed from the colours on the Brazilian flag and is carried on the wings and fuselage of most FAB aircraft. The exceptions are the Mirages and F-5Es which have the marking only on the wings in miniature form against, respectively, blue-grey and three-tone Vietnam-style camouflage. On tactical aircraft a small yellow-green flash is carried on the fin, while non-camouflaged support and training types have these colours painted on the rudders, usually to the full width and depth. Unit or Grupo badges are also carried, usually on the fin or nose, and transport aircraft bear FORCA AEREA BRASILEIRA on the fuselage.

viana for a number of years, as attempts to replace them with more modern Mirage 50s have been thwarted by financial problems. In their place, the French have agreed to supply 18 ex-French Air Force Lockheed T-33s to add to some Canadian examples supplied in the early 1970s. FAB aircraft carry the roundel marking on the wings and fuselage, together with the national colours applied across the rudder in equal segments with red at the top. Black numbers (eg, 651, 652, 656)

are painted on the fin of both natural metal and camouflaged Sabres, while support and training aircraft such as the PC-7s have large numbers on the fuselage prefixed FAB. Badges and flamboyant nose markings (shark mouths and eagle's heads) feature on many FAB aircraft, but particularly the PC-7s, of which 24 have been purchased. Transport aircraft carry registrations in the series TAM-01 (TAM for Transportes Aéreos Militares) and provide national passenger services.

Serialling is in four-digit number blocks, the first number indicating the basic role:

0 and 1 — training; 2 — transport; 3 — liaison; 4 — fighter; 5 — bomber; 6 — amphibian; 7 — maritime patrol; 8 — helicopters.

The other three digits represent the individual aircraft and the last two are repeated larger on the nose. Every Brazilian military aircraft is given a type designation and this also appears on the fin as a prefix to the number. Current examples are as shown.

Anomalies occur in this system. The Bandeirante patrol version is prefixed P and the reconnaissance version R; while the rescue variant is known as the SC-95.

The Brazilian Navy is a helicopter operator (fixed-wing types such as the carrier-borne Trackers coming under FAB control) and employs a green-yellow-blue roundel as its standard insignia. Serials are prefixed N and are carried on the tail booms of the Sea Kings, Lynx and Ecureuils, while MARINHA in bold letters identifies naval machines.

Above: A Brazilian Air Force F-5F combat trainer displaying the national star marking under both wings and the centrally mounted fin flash.

Brazilian type designations

C-91	HS.748
C-93	HS.125
C-95	EMB-110 Bandeirante
C-96	Boeing 737
C-115	DHC-5 Buffalo
C-130	Lockheed C-130 Hercules
F-5	Northrop F-5E
F-103	Dassault Mirage III
H-4	Bell 206
H-13	Bell 47
H-33	Aérospatiale SA.330 Puma
L-42	Neiva Regente
P-16	Grumman S-2E Tracker
T-23	Aerotec 122 Uirapuru
T-25	Neiva Universal
T-26	EMB.326 Xavante
T-27	EMB.312 Tucano
U-7	EMB.810 Seneca II
U-9	EMB.121 Xingu
U-19	EMB.201 Ipanema

Bulgaria

combat aircraft (MiG-17, MiG-21 and MiG-23) and on the fins of transport types such as the An-24. Although LZ is the civilian registration, most military transports also carry this prefix along with a three- or four-digit number. Examples are LZ-1126, an An-2, and LZ-093, an AN-24.

Using the Soviet red star as its basis, the Bulgarian national insignia has the national colours at its centre. In this form it is located on the wings and fuselage of Bulgarian Air Force

Below: Red four-digit identification numbers are prominent on these Bulgarian MiG-21MF fighters while their pilots indulge in a 'line-shoot'.

Burma

identity. They are sometimes prefixed UB for Union of Burma and are often applied in Burmese numerals:

0	1	2	3	4
0	၁	J	၃	၄

5	6	7	8	9
၅	၆	၇	၈	၉

Known as Tamdaw Lay, the Burmese air arm is principally a counter-insurgency force equipped with a handful of Lockheed AT-33As, 16 armed Pilatus PC-7 trainers and about nine SF.260 Warriors. The triangular marking, which bears no relation to the Burmese national flag, is carried on the fuselage and wings. Aircraft have a serial number which serves as both unit and individual

Recent examples are: Lockheed AT-33As 3520, 3526; PC-7s 2301-2316; Bell UH-1Hs 6201-6218; and Alouette IIIs 6101-6114. The numbers are sometimes split on the fuselage by the national insignia and applied in white on a camouflaged background, or painted close together on the aft fuselage in black on light finishes.

Cameroun

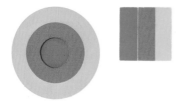

This former French colony gained independence in 1960 and established a small air arm, 'Armée de l'Air du Cameroun, operating some transport and liaison aircraft. A counter-insurgency element was subsequently added in the form of four Potez Magisters, these being replaced by six Alpha Jets in 1984. The national marking is formed from the pan-African colours and when used as rudder striping, with green leading, a yellow star of liberty is applied centrally on the red segment. Aircraft carry a registration in the TJ-XAA to -XZZ block, examples being Lockheed C-130H TJ-XAC, Alpha Jet TJ-XBV and DHC-5 Buffalo TJ-XBT. Unit badges are worn on the noses of the Hercules, and this type has the words CAMEROON AIR FORCES applied in red on the forward fuselage.

Canada

Standard

Low-visibility

As an important member of NATO, Canada stations equipment in West Germany and the air element, known as the 1st Canadian Air Group, currently comprises CF-18 Hornets based at Baden-Söllingen together with some CH-136 Kiowa liaison helicopters at Lahr. Based in Canada are more of the 138 Hornets currently being delivered to replace the CF-104s, some CF-116 fighter/trainers and 18 CP-140 Aurora maritime patrol aircraft. Supporting these tactical elements is a strong force of transports, helicopters and training aircraft.

The maple leaf insignia was adopted by the Royal Canadian Air Force after the end of World War I. In slightly modified form it continues to be the national marking of what is now known as the Canadian Armed Forces — Air and is carried in low visibility form on the wings and fuselage of the present equipment. Under Canadian law, titling in English has to be repeated in French and *vice versa*, hence ARMED FORCES — FORCES ARMEES applied either side of the fuselage roundel on CAF aircraft. On the Hornets, the word CANADA is carried mid-way along the fuselage, while on the outside of the fins is the national flag insignia in dark grey together with the serial number. Unit badges are painted unobtrusively on the fin tips, again in dark grey against the light grey camouflage background. Canada is the only country to have officially adopted a scheme experimented with by a number of western air forces, the painting of a false cockpit on the underside of the nose of its Hornets. This takes the form of a dark grey outline aligned with the pilot's canopy. The individual aircraft number is applied under the port wing, and CAF under the starboard, mid-way between tip and root.

Canadian military aircraft are given a type designation comprising a role prefix, preceded in all cases by the letter C, and followed by a sequential number. Current examples are as listed in the table on the following page. ▶

Canadian type designations

CF-104	Canadair CF-104
CH-113	Vertol 107
CT-114	Canadair CL-41 Tutor
CC-115	DHC-5 Buffalo
CF-116	Northrop CF-5
CC-117	Dassault Falcon 20
CH-118	Bell UH-1H
CH-124	Sikorsky S-61
CC-130	Lockheed C-130 Hercules
CC-132	DHC-7 Dash Seven
CT-134	Beech Musketeer
CH-135	Bell UH-1N
CH-136	Bell OH-58 Kiowa
CC-137	Boeing 707
CC-138	DHC-6 Twin Otter
CH-139	Bell 206B
CP-140	Lockheed P-3 Aurora
CC-144	Canadair Challenger
CH-147	Vertol CH-47C
CF-188	CF-18 Hornet

Serial numbers normally carried on the aircraft tail incorporate the designation but omit the letter prefix and are followed by a sequential number of up to three digits. Thus 188745 signifies a CF-18 assigned the serial number 745, which is often repeated on the aircraft nose as well as under the port wing.

Chad

The Escadrille Nationale Tchadienne was formed with French assistance in 1973 and operated six Douglas Skyraiders for some years before a civil war, attrition and the general vulnerability of these old piston-engined bombers forced their withdrawal. Since then, the air arm is known to have received two Pilatus PC-7s armed with underwing guns, but probably no other combat aircraft. Transports constitute the main type of equipment; among the types in current service are nine C-47s, three DC-4s, two Noratlas, two C-130A Hercules and a single Caravelle 6R, the last used for VIP duties. There are also ten Alouette III and four SA.330 Puma helicopters. Aircraft are allocated registrations prefixed TT.

Chile

Air Force

Navy

Low-visibility

Chilean military aircraft carry the main components of the national flag in the form of a white star on a shield

Above: Canada plans to have 138 CF-18s. These two-seaters of 410 Sqn are in standard toned-down colours (FS 35237 blue-grey on upper surface, FS 36118 dark grey for false canopy).

Central African Republic

Originally part of French Equatorial Africa, this relatively poor country allocates only a minimal sum to defence and its air arm. The latter's main tasks are civil assistance flights using C-47s and Macchi AL60 transports. Military aircraft operated by the Force Aérienne Centrafricaine are allocated designations from TL-KAA. Civil types also carry the TL prefix. No combat aircraft are on strength at present, an order for 12 Pucaras having been cancelled.

in blue and red, representing the snow on the Andes mountains, the sky above and the blood shed by the nation's patriots. In this form it is usually located only above the starboard wing and under the port wing, the opposite positions being occupied by the individual aircraft

Above: Chilean Air Force A-37B light attack aircraft showing the positioning of the wing insignia and individual aircraft number.

number. The white star appears on the rudder of all aircraft, either over the camouflage or on a specially ▶

painted dark blue background. There are exceptions to every rule, and the two Boeing 707s operated by the Fuerza Aerea de Chile have a large white star applied in the centre of the all-blue fin and rudder. They also have the air force title painted along the fuselage.

Fuerza Aerea de Chile aircraft are allocated serials in blocks; jet-powered aircraft have J prefixes to three-digit numbers.

Helicopters have serials beginning with H, while other types wear un-prefixed numbers in the following ranges: trainers 100 and 400, light transports 200, medium transports 300 and miscellaneous aircraft and

FAeCh jet aircraft serials

J-500-515	Dassault Mirage 50 interceptors
J-600-	Cessna A-37B close-support aircraft
J-700-	Hawker Hunter fighters
J-800-817	Northrop F-5E/F fighters
J-370-	Cessna T-37B/C trainers

Colombia

The multi-coloured national insignia, applied to Colombian military aircraft for more than 40 years, bears little resemblance to the country's flag. The horizontal rudder striping is a closer representation, this being carried on all aircraft operated by the Fuerza Aerea Colombiana, the red and yellow colours symbolising the nation's Spanish origins.

The roundel is carried on the fuselage and wings of most types, in-cluding the Mirage 5s — 14 5COA fighters, two 5COR reconnaissance aircraft and two 5COD trainers being delivered in 1972 — and on the sur-viving Lockheed AT-33s of more than 50 received. Cessna A-37Bs operate in the attack role, painted in dark disruptive camouflage of dark green, tan and black. All aircraft carry FAC on their fins above the serial number, the latter being repeated under the port wing and above the starboard wing. The roundel ocupies the opposite posi-tion on the wings.

Serials are allocated in three- and four-digit blocks, examples being FAC 902 on a Douglas DC-6 and 3023 on a Mirage 5COA fighter. A suffix letter applied to a serial indicates a replacement aircraft for one lost (eg,

heavy transports 900. The serial number features prominently on the rear fuselage or tail of most types. One anomaly with the above system is the apparent numbering of the three ex-RAF Canberra PR.9s, delivered to the FAeCh in 1982, as 341, 342 and 343. As these are hardly medium transports, the whole system would appear subject to variation.

Chilean naval aircraft, including six EMB.111ANS for maritime patrol plus Bandeirante transports and Lynx ASW helicopters, carry the insignia with anchor motif.

306A on a T-34). Numbers in the 1100 to 1199 block are reserved for aircraft operated by the military airline, Satena, which flies a number of types on internal routes within Colombia. FUERZA AEREA COLOMBIANA is normally applied to the fuselages of transport aircraft and the rear booms of helicopters, while the majority of stencilling is in Spanish such as HELICE for propeller and RESCATE for rescue.

Below: The ninth Mirage 5COA delivered to the Fuerza Aérea Colombiana. The roundel on the fuselage is distorted by an engine intake door, while the red and yellow patch on the forward part of the wing marks an airbrake.

China

The Air Force of the People's Liberation Army is the third largest air arm in the world with an estimated strength of some 4,750 aircraft. It is organized along Soviet lines with up to four squadrons, each with about 15 aircraft, forming an Air Regiment, and three Regiments making up an Air Division. Yet by Western standards the AFPLA is equipped largely with obsolete aircraft dating back to the 1960s, when Soviet designs began to be produced. The MiG-19 forms the backbone of the Chinese fighter force, which knows it as the Jian-6, and some 40 Regiments fly the type. A more modern aircraft is the Chinese version of the Soviet MiG-21 designate 1 Jian-7. The only other single-seat aircraft operational in any quantity is the Qiang-5 attack aircraft, developed from the J-6 but with side intakes and eight attachment points for external stores.

The Chinese national star and bar marking is carried on all these aircraft and on the H-5 (Il-28) and H-6 (Tu-16) bombers, located prominently on each side of the rear fuselage and on the wings. The central motif of the star contains the Chinese characters 8 over 1. Code numbers on the noses and on engine nacelles of military aircraft are formed of five digits, often in stencil-split style, and painted in a number of colours including red, black and yellow. Most fighter and attack aircraft appear to be unpainted, although some examples of the Qiang-5 carry a green disruptive camouflage over the top surfaces. Also observed on the Qiang-5 is an unusual marking combination painted on the outside of the large wing fence and on the fuselage. This is believed to be intended for formation flying: viewed from the rear three-quarter position, the two designs merge to form one.

Congo

The small Congolese air arm — l'Armée de l'Air du Congo — received a token combat element of MiG-15s and -17s from the Soviet Union following independence in 1960. These may not be operational, the air force having assumed a predominantly transport character with the arrival of some ex-French Noratlas to join existing An-24s and C-47s. The roundel is applied to the wings and fuselage, while a fin flash is a replica of the national flag. Aircraft serials are prefixed TN and have three digits.

Cuba

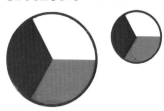

Operating equipment almost entirely supplied by the Soviet Union, the Fuerza Aérea Revolucionaria indulges in hardly any spectacular colouring on its combat aircraft. The roundel marking is carried on the wings and fuselage of most aircraft and the rudder striping is a repeat of the national flag but incorporating an isosceles triangle with a small star on the trailing edge.

The US Department of Defense estimates that there are some 450 aircraft in service with the FAR, the combat units flying MiG-17s, MiG-21s and some of the latest MiG-23s. Photographs have revealed that some of the MiG-21s continue to operate in natural metal, while the swing-wing MiG-23s bear a camouflage finish, presumably applied prior to delivery from the Soviet factory. Although confirmation is still needed, it can be assumed that the Mil Mi-24 gunship helicopters have a disruptive green camouflage with light grey undersides in a similar style to that used on Nicaraguan-flown examples.

FAR serialling appears somewhat haphazard. Numbers carried on the MiG-21s range between 103 and 663 and the MiG-17s are in the 200-range, while one MiG-23 is 710. Tactical transports such as the fleet of 20 An-24s have four-digit serials over the green pattern camouflage.

Czechoslovakia

A Communist state since May 1948, Czechoslovakia is a member of the Warsaw Pact and as such has a combat force within the Ceskoslovenske Letectvo (Czech Air Force) of Soviet-supplied aircraft. Numerically, the most important type in service is the MiG-21, with more than 300 operated in the fighter, reconnaissance and training roles. MiG-23s in both fighter and ground-attack versions total about 80, supported by older types such as the Sukhoi Su-7 and MiG-17. In 1985 about 20 of the latest Su-25 close support aircraft joined the air arm, to date the only operator of the type outside the Soviet Union. More than 20 Mi-24 attack helicopters are also in use.

Since they are used in tactical roles, almost all front-line Czech Air

Force aircraft are camouflaged in green and brown disruptive schemes with light blue underneath. Over this is applied the national marking, formed from the colours of the former Austrian provinces of Bohemia (red and white) and Moravia (blue). It is located above and below each wing and on both sides of the fin with blue foremost. Serials are usually applied on the forward fuselage in black, although MiG-23s have been seen carrying the four-digit number on the intakes in black outlined in white. Mi-24s also have four-figure numbers, but carried on the rear tail booms.

Personal or unit markings are almost unheard of in the East European air forces, but in the mid-1970s one MiG-21 was seen with a black and white chequered rudder and a small emblem on the nose showing a wolf's head on a green shield. This attempt at introducing some sort of individualism into the Service appears not to have been repeated.

Below: A Czech MiG-23MF 'Flogger-B' in disruptive green/brown camouflage. Its black four-digit identification number, outlined in white, is on the side of the engine intake.

Denmark

This NATO country operates a combat force of more than 40 Saab 35 Drakens and 50 General Dynamics F-16s. The Drakens are assigned to the attack role and are camouflaged in non-reflective dark olive drab and light grey, with low-visibility roundels and fin flashes. The F-16s are tasked with air defence and carry the standard factory finish of three greys together with miniature markings. The red and white markings have

been used on Danish military aircraft since the First World War and the fin flash is a representation of the national flag or *Dannebrog*.

Every Royal Danish Air Force (Kongelige Danske Flyvevåbnet) aircraft carries an individual letter/number code comprising one or two prefix letters followed by a three-digit number. This number is formed from the last three digits of the aircraft's construction number. An example is Draken A-008 which was built by Saab and given the c/n 351008. The codes and serials of the present RDAF combat force are as shown (see overleaf).

RDAF transport and training aircraft often carry the Service badge on the forward fuselage, while Lynx helicopters operated by the Danish ▶

Royal Danish Air Force aircraft codes

Saab F35 Draken	A-001 to A-020	Attack aircraft
Saab RF35 Draken	AR-101 to AR-120	Reconnaissance aircraft
Saab TF35 Draken	AT-151 to AT-161	Combat trainers
General Dynamics F-16A	E-174 to E-611	Interceptors
General Dynamics F-16B	ET-204 to ET-615	Combat trainers

Naval Air Service carry an anchor insignia on the cabin. The latter are operated from frigates of the Danish Navy and carry the serials S-134, -142, -170, -175, -181, -187, -191 and -196.

Below: ET-205 is a Danish F-16B, seen here armed with two practice Sidewinders. National markings are in standard miniaturized form; the radome was later sprayed Middle Grey.

Dominica

About six surviving de Havilland Vampire F.1/FB.50s constitute the only jet-powered combat element of the Fuerza Aérea Dominicana,

although the serviceability of these ageing aircraft must be marginal. The Dominican roundel is based on the national flag and is carried on the fuselage as well as on the top surface of the port wing and the lower surface of the starboard wing. The letters FAD are applied to the fin above the aircraft serial number, the Vampires being numbered between 2701 and 2742. A green and tan camouflage finish has been applied to the aircraft.

Ecuador

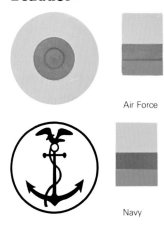

Air Force

Navy

Rather confusingly, Ecuador has a national flag almost identical to that of neighbouring Colombia, the only differences being in the shade of blue and the proportions of the flag. On aircraft flown by the Ecuadorian Air Force (Fuerza Aérea Ecuatoriana) both the roundel and the rudder or fin flash have the colours in proportions directly related to those of the flag.

Ecuador has one of the best equipped air arms in the area and is able to field Mirage F.1s, Jaguar fighter-bombers, Kfir interceptors and Strikemaster and A-37B Dragonfly attack aircraft. Most of these types are camouflaged, some in the air force's own adopted style of brown and tan, and others in green/grey (Jaguars) or green/brown (Mirage F.1s). The roundel is normally applied above the port wing and below the starboard wing, the opposite positions being occupied by the letters FAE in black and, in some cases, the aircraft serial number. FAE aircraft generally use the construction number or the last three digits of it as their identification serial.

Transport aircraft carry FUERZA AEREA ECUATORIANA somewhere on the fuselage alongside the civil registration on the fin alongside the military serial number. Ecuadorian registrations are prefixed HC. Some FAE aircraft carry prefixes to the serial such as BE for the currently withdrawn Canberras, and TP for the Cessna T-41D trainers. Badges are sometimes worn, usually on the nose, to denote the operating unit.

Air elements of the Ecuadorian Army carry the name EJERCITO, while Navy-operated aircraft have NAVAL in prominent letters on the fuselage, an anchor motif on the fin and serials prefixed ANE. Both these Services carry roundels on the wings together with the relevant serials, in the same style as FAE machines.

Below: Ecuador's Jaguars were all delivered in standard RAF green/grey camouflage. Only the fin marking identifies the user.

Egypt

The Arab Republic of Egypt maintains a diverse spread of equipment obtained from behind the Iron Curtain as well as from sources in the Far East and the West. Surviving Soviet aircraft operated by the Egyptian Air Force (Al Quwwat al Jawwiya il-Misriya), supplied prior to the October 1973 war with Israel, comprise more than 100 MiG-21s, nearly 70 Su-7/20s, of which approximately 20 are operational, about 20 MiG-19s and 70 MiG-17s. The severing of diplomatic relations with the Soviet Union at the time of the war produced a critical spares shortage which was subsequently overcome by western equipment companies, which supplied many replacements for original Soviet parts to keep the force viable.

To build up the EAF in the late 1970s China agreed to provide 80 F-6 (MiG-19) and 60 F-7 (MiG-21) interceptors, and these are being integrated into the air force. The United States, another of the countries Egypt turned to for new equip-

Below: Under Peace Vector, Egypt received 9301, the first of 80 F-16s, in early 1982. The aircraft carry basic insignia and standard Middle Grey/Underbelly Grey colours.

ment, supplied 35 F-4E Phantoms as stop-gap fighters pending the arrival of the first of 40 F-16s (the Phantoms were still in service at the beginning of 1986), while from France 40 Mirage 2000s have been ordered to replace the Mirage 5s originally paid for by Saudi Arabia and operated by the EAF. For the ground-attack role, Alpha Jets are being built in Egypt with an initial order for 15 currently being fulfilled.

All these aircraft carry the EAF roundel on wings and fuselage, while on the fin is a small reproduction of the national flag. Serials are formed of four numbers applied in Arabic style on the nose or, in the case of the Mirages, on the rear fuselage. Unit badges are rare, although small designs have been noted on some MiG-21s, and the Mirage 5s have carried large orange-painted areas on their wings and tails since the 1973 war. These were outlined in black and almost duplicated a similar design painted on Israeli-operated Mirage IIIs during the conflict. The precise reason for this apparent copying had not been determined at the time of writing: it is presumed that the EAF decided the design was so distinctive to ground troops that they would hold their fire against these aircraft at low altitude.

Below: F-4E Phantom, USAF serial 66-0366, has Egyptian serial 7813 in Arabic script on the nose. The sale of Egypt's Phantoms to Turkey has been rumoured for some time.

0	1	2	3	4
.	١	٢	٣	٤
5	6	7	8	9
٥,	٦	٧	٨	٩

60366

VAIV

Ethiopia

The Ethiopian Air Force roundel is formed from the colours of the national flag and is applied in the standard positions on each EAF aircraft. The serial numbers applied on the fins do not appear to follow any logical sequence, three de Havilland Doves obtained many years ago being numbered 801-803 and four Canberra B.52 bombers bought in the late 1960s carrying 351-354. It is unlikely that these machines are still in service, the operational strength of the air force lying in a number of squadrons equipped with more than 100 MiG-21 fighters and MiG-23 fighter-bombers supplied to the present Marxist government by the Soviet Union. These aircraft and a number of Mi-24 attack helicopters are engaged in a war with the Eritrean Liberation Front guerrillas. Other types known to be in use include six An-12s, some An-26s, ten SF.260TP two-seat trainers and some Alouette III helicopters bought from India.

Finland

The present Finnish Air Force (Ilmavoimat) roundel replaced the original blue swastika on a white field toward the end of World War II. It now adorns all Finnish military aircraft and helicopters. Under the terms of the 1947 Treaty of Paris, the Finnish AF is officially limited to a strength of 60 combat aircraft. The three air defence wings which currently make up the air arm are equip-

ped with 27 Saab J35 Drakens and 30 MiG-21s. A further 18 Drakens are on order from Sweden for delivery in 1986. Nearly 50 Hawks are in service in the training role, taking student pilots from the initial course on the small Valmet Vinkas, before passing them on to the squadrons for type conversion.

The Finnish system of identifying aircraft consists of a two-letter prefix denoting the aircraft type, followed by a sequential number of up to three digits. This marking is carried on the rear fuselage or helicopter tail boom. Both the Drakens and the MiG-21s carry a disruptive camouflage scheme over the top surfaces of dark green and dark grey with light grey on the undersides.

Finnish Air Force identification serials

Saab J35 Draken	DK-201 to 271 (27 in service by late-1985)
MiG-21bis/UM	MG-111 to 144 (29 'bis' and two UM)
BAe Hawk T.51	HW-301 to 350
Fokker F.27-100 Friendship	FF-1 to FF-3
Potez CM.170 Magister	FM-1 to 82 (small number remain in use)
VL Vinka	VN-1 to 30

France

Air Force

Navy

It is to France that credit should be given for establishing a basic form of military aircraft marking: on July 26, 1912, an official French Army order decreed that roundels should be applied to the wings and fuselage of all military flying machines. The concentric rings of red, white and blue laid down then have survived to the present day. From 1945, a narrow yellow outline was added to ensure that the marking stood out against camouflage paint or the natural metal finish retained by many aircraft in the post-war years, but in 1982 French military aircraft, like those of other Western air forces, underwent a toning-down process whereby the roundel diminished in size — from 80cm to 58cm in the case of the Mirage III, for example — and lost its yellow surround.

Rudder stripes, which also originated before World War I, began to disappear from French combat aircraft in the early 1970s, although examples can still be seen applied to second-line types. The stripes are carried in the order blue/white/red from front to rear on both sides of the tail. The aircraft manufacturer, mark

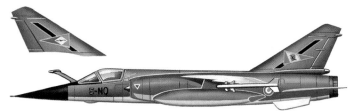

Above: 5 Escadre de Chasse at Orange was the second Wing to equip with the Mirage F.1. This

F.1C-200 has the two escadrille badges on the fin, SPA124 (Joan of Arc) port and SPA26 (stork).

Above: A Jaguar of the fourth squadron of Escadre de Chasse 11, operating from Toul and

Bordeaux. The fin carries the two escadrille badges and on the intake is the Wing number.

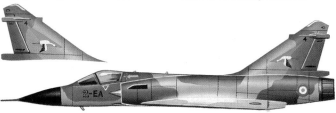

Above: It was predictable that EC2 at Dijon, the famous Cigognes Wing, would be the

first unit to receive the Mirage 2000 interceptor. Note the rear location of the fuselage roundel.

number and construction number may be stencilled in black on the rudder and often over the stripes.

Coloured badges are also painted on the fin. Usually a different one is carried on each side, reflecting current Armée de l'Air unit organisation. An Escadre, composed of up to four Escadrons, is the basic unit; each Escadron is formed by two Escadrilles, and it is the badges of both these elements which are normally displayed on either side. For example, the 12 Escadre de Chasse is made up of EC1/12, EC2/12 and EC3/12: Mirage F1.Cs of EC1/12 would carry the codes 12-YA to 12-YZ on their noses, the number indicating the Escadre, Y the first Escadron and the final letter being

the individual aircraft in the escadron. The number is often applied stencil-split in black outline followed by the letters in stencil-split solid black. In this case the left-hand side of the fin would carry a hornet of SPA89 while the right-hand has a tiger's head of SPA162, the first and second Escadrilles respectively.

Rescue and maintenance information around the airframe takes the form of standard NATO markings and these too have undergone changes to reduce their visibility. Ejection seat markings are now generally applied in red and black with the white deleted, while the prominent red/yellow wing-walk markings on the wings of Mirages have had the yellow deleted. ▶

Above: One of the three squadrons forming EC5 at Orange operates as a conversion unit for all French Air Force Mirage F.1 Wings. This two-seat F.1B combat trainer carries a large Super 530 air-to-air missile underwing and a dummy Magic round on the wingtip. Behind the Wing number and individual aircraft letters are the two ejection seat triangles, while behind the rear cockpit are the ground rescue instructions.

Left: French Army Gazelle and Puma helicopters have recently adopted the legend 'armee de TERRE' on their rear tailbooms. As this example of the former type shows, the roundel is retained. Leaving the launch tube of this SA. 342M is a HOT wire-guided anti-tank missile.

Aéronavale

The French Naval Air Arm has a front-line force of Super Etendards, Etendards, F-8E(FN) Crusaders, Atlantics, Alizés, Super Frelons and Lynx helicopters. Units operating these types are numbered and carry a suffix letter F for *Flotille*. Second-line units carry the suffix S for *Escadrille de Servitude*. Examples are 14F, which flies Super Etendards from Landivisiau, and 11S, equipped with Xingu transports at Dugny.

Naval aircraft carry roundels on the wings and fuselage with a black anchor superimposed. In 1984, a two-tone grey colour scheme was tested on Super Etendards and Etendards, with the result that the roundel lost its yellow outline and the individual aircraft number was changed from white to grey. Note that Aéronavale aircraft carry the wing roundel only on the upper left ▶

and lower right surfaces; in the other positions is the aircraft number. This is principally for ease of identification during carrier operations.

The legend MARINE can be applied on the aft fuselage in black (eg Crusaders) or white (eg Lynx and Super Frelon). Unit badges tend to be less flamboyant in application on naval aircraft than those on AdlA machines; when carried, their usual positions are under the cockpit (Crusader) and at the base of the leading edge of the fin (Super Etendard).

Aviation Légère de l'Armée de Terre

French Army Aviation is mainly composed of Gazelle and Alouette II/III light helicopters plus Puma trans-

Above: Prompted by experience in the Lebanon in 1983-84, the Aéronavale has adopted a random disruptive blue-grey camouflage for its Super Etendards. Aircraft No 70 has its fuselage roundel obscured.

port/troop carriers. The machines are allocated to military units at divisional level and only a few markings are carried. The most prominent of these is the three-letter code indicating the individual peloton or escadrille, usually carried each side of the main cabin, and ARMEE DE TERRE applied along the tail booms of most of the Gazelles and Pumas currently in use. A small roundel is usually carried towards the rear of the main cabin.

French callsign blocks in current use

F-BAAA to -BZZZ	Civil flying registrations. Series used since 1940
F-CAAA to -CZZZ	Current gliders
F-MAAA to -MZZZ	Army Aviation (Aviation Légère de l'Armée de Terre)
F-MJAA to -MJZZ	Gendarmerie or Police-operated aircraft and helicopters
F-MMAA to -MMZZ	Army Aviation (ALAT)
F-OAAA to -OZZZ	French overseas civil aircraft
F-PAAA to -PZZZ	Provisional civil registrations
F-RAAA to -ULZZ	Armée de l'Air
F-VAAA to -VAZZ	Civil delivery flights
F-WAAA to -WZZZ	Experimental and prototype aircraft/helicopters
F-XAAA to -YZZZ	Aéronavale
F-ZAAA to -ZAZZ	Aircraft/helicopters under evaluation
F-ZBAA to -ZBBZ	Protection Civile
F-ZBCA to -ZWZZ	State organizations, trials and support aircraft

Gabon

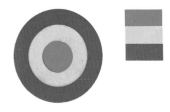

About a dozen Dassault Mirage 5 fighter-bombers acquired by the Forces Aériennes Gabonaises constitute the country's front-line combat strength. While some were ordered as new-build aircraft, later machines were supplied from ex-Libyan stocks and include some two-seat Mirage 5DG trainers. These aircraft carry a disruptive camouflage scheme of green and grey over their top surfaces with the Gabon roundel on the intake sides and the wings. Three-digit identification serials are carried. Hercules transport aircraft of the FAG have the full name of the air force applied on the forward fuselage and a civilian registration painted on the fin, TR-KKB and TR-KKC being two examples. Prominently displayed at the top of the fin is a reproduction of the national flag. VIP aircraft have the legend REPUBLIQUE GABONAISE on the sides of the fuselage.

Germany (East)

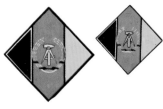

The German Democratic Republic has existed since 1948, when it was formed from the Soviet-occupied eastern zone of Germany. An air arm was established under the title DDR Luftstreitkräfte und Luftverteidigung and integrated with the Warsaw Pact Command structure. The combat aircraft operated by the LSK/LV are all standard Soviet designs, East Germany having given up its attempts to establish its own aircraft manufacturing industry in the 1960s. The MiG-21 is numerically the most important aircraft type in service and operates in both the fighter and ground-attack roles. Camouflaged and natural metal examples have been noted, with three-digit numbers on the nose, usually in black. While the single-seat MiG-21s, of which there are some 250 in service, carry numbers ranging between 400 and 980, two-seat MiG-21U and UM trainers are almost always seen in the 200 series.

More than 90 MiG-23s are in service, some as dedicated interceptors and others as close support aircraft fitted with laser noses and external attachment points for various air-to-ground ordnance. Both versions appear to be camouflaged in green and brown with numbers between 500 and 800 in red or black on the forward fuselage. Helicopters include Mi-24s painted in disruptive camouflage for the low-level attack role, and dark green Mi-8 assault machines, all marked with serials on the tail booms.

The national marking is prominently displayed on the wings and fins of fixed-wing aircraft and on the rear cabins of helicopters. The central emblem in the diamond consists of symbols representing the nation's working people.

In structure and deployment the LSK/LV follows the pattern of a Soviet Air Army, with combat units grouped in divisions and separate support regiments; fighter units for instance, are grouped in divisions, as are the SAM units which are integrated with the Soviet air defence network. The East German Air Force headquarters at Strausberg-Eggersdorf controls the 1st Air Defence Division, with an HQ at Cottbus, and the 3rd ADD, headquartered at Neubrandenburg.

The East German Navy has a small helicopter force equipped with Mi-14 ASW and minesweeping machines.

Germany (West)

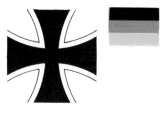

The familiar iron cross of the West German Air Force, or Luftwaffe, bears a close similarity to that displayed on aircraft dating back to World War I and was adopted in the mid-1950s when the re-formed air arm was constituted. A miniature national flag was also chosen for the fin flash. Since 1968 Luftwaffe aircraft have been identified by four-digit serial numbers, usually split by the national marking. The current range is divided into serial blocks allocated to aircraft roles.

Luftwaffe serial blocks

0001-0999	Experimental aircraft
1001-1999	VIP and staff transports
2001-4999	Front-line combat aircraft
5001-5999	Transport aircraft
6001-6999	Maritime patrol aircraft
7001-7999	Light helicopters
8001-8999	Medium helicopters
9001-9999	Trainers

Under this system, in whiich the numbers are usually sequential, McDonnell Douglas RF-4E Phantom 35 + 03 is the third machine of the type obtained by the service. A total of 88 of these reconnaissance Phantoms were bought.

The Luftwaffe currently operates five main types of combat aircraft: Panavia Tornado (all-weather strike), F-4F and RF-4E Phantom (fighter-bomber and reconnaissance), Lockheed F-104G Starfighter (fighter-bomber) and Dassault-Breguet/Dornier Alpha Jet (light attack/close-support). The Starfighters are scheduled to be replaced by Tornados, of which 212 have been ordered, and to maintain the effectiveness of the F-4s an improvement programme is well under way to keep

Above: Luftwaffe Tornado 44 + 43 of JaboG 32 which converted from F-104G Starfighters in 1984. This aircraft carries the new dark grey, dark green and medium green colour scheme although the pylon and fuel tank remain in the old colours. The unit shield is applied to both sides of the fin, but note that the national markings are on the port upper and starboard lower wings only.

them operational until their replacements arrive in the late 1990s. The codes and badges applied to each of these major warplanes and the units operating them are detailed on page 44.

The camouflage schemes used on Luftwaffe aircraft are detailed in the chapter on the subject. Note that all German military aircraft carry standard NATO maintenance, rescue and servicing markings (see the United Kingdom entry for examples), some in toned-down form to reduce brightness on the later types of camouflage.

Bundesmarine

The West German naval air arm combines fixed-wing combat aircraft (Tornados and remaining Starfighters)

with ASW aircraft (Atlantics) and SAR/ASV helicopters (Lynx and Sea Kings). The service has a distinctive camouflage scheme of basalt grey (RAL7012) and pale grey (RAL7035) and its aircraft wear the black anchor symbol together with the legend MARINE.

Marinefliegergeschwader 1, or MFG 1, is based at Schleswig and flies ▶

Above: The badge identifies this F-4F Phantom as being from JaboG 36 at Hopsten. Partly hidden by the intake splitter plate are the dual language (German and English) rescue instructions which are applied to all aircraft operated by NATO. The beige marking at lower right is a low-light formation strip.

Luftwaffe combat units, aircraft serials and badges

Panavia Tornado: 43 + 01 to 44 + 53 to date

JaboG 31 'Boelcke'	Winged sword on shield
JaboG 32	Bird with bomb insignia

McDonnell Douglas F-4F Phantom: 37 + 01 to 38 + 75

JaboG 35	Eagle's head emblem
JaboG 36	Prancing horse in shield
JG 71 'Richthofen'	Red R on white shield
JG 74 'Molders'	Paper dart on circular shield

McDonnell Douglas RF-4E Phantom: 35 + 01 to 35 + 88

AG 51 'Immelmann'	Owl emblem
AG 52	Panther head

Lockheed F-104G Starfighter: 20 + 01 to 26 + 90

JaboG 33	Stylized bird on lozenge-shaped shield
JaboG 34	Two paper darts over mountains on shield

Alpha Jet: 40 + 01 to 41 + 75

JaboG 41	Eagle's head in outline
JaboG 43	Two darts and Viking ship prow
JaboG 44	Lion and NATO symbol
JaboG 49	Diving eagle and lightning flash

JaboG 35 is equipped with F-4Fs and based at Pferdsfeld.

JaboG 36 has some 46 Phantoms on strength.

JG 71 carries the famous Richthofen badge on its F-4Fs.

JG 74 is named after World War II ace Werner Molders.

AG 51 'Immelmann' provides all-weather recce via RF-4Es.

AG 52, sister unit to AG 51, also has RF-4Es.

JaboG 31 'Boelcke' has Tornados at Norvenich.

JaboG 32, also a Tornado unit, flies from Lechfeld.

JaboG 33 has F-104Gs but will receive Tornados.

Tornados in the strike role. Each aircraft in the wing carries the unit emblem (a diving eagle over the sea) at the top of each side of the fin. The other combat unit is MFG 2 at Eggebek, whose more than 50 F-104G/TF-104G Starfighters will be replaced by Tornados shortly; the unit badge is a figure 2 on a gunsight marking. The Atlantics are based at Nordholz and have codes from 61+01 to 61+20. Neither they nor the helicopters operated by MFG 5 at Kiel carried their unit badges at the time of writing.

Left: MarinefliegerGeschwader 5 based at Kiel operates Lynx ASW helicopters, of which 83+02, seen here 'dunking' its sonar, was the second machine of an order for 14. The national marking can just be seen on top of the rotor housing and the word MARINE is carried in black on the rear tail boom. MFG 5 also uses Sea Kings and Do28s.

Ghana

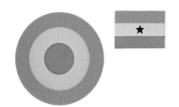

Aermacchi MB.326 jet trainers, some armed, form the only 'combat' aircraft currently in service with the Ghana Air Force. Finished in a disruptive camouflage and delivered with broad yellow bands round the rear fuselage, these aircraft can be expected to be replaced in the near future, financial resources permitting. Serials run from G700 and there are believed to be about ten survivors of the 14 originally received. GAF aircrat all carry three-digit serials prefixed G (other types in use are F.27 Friendship and Short Skyvan transports, and SF.260TP trainers) and national roundels and fin flashes are applied in the usual positions, though the single F.28 Fellowship carries the flashes on the engine nacelles.

Greece

The Hellenic Air Force, or Polemikí Aeroporía, forms part of NATO's 6th ATAF defending the vulnerable southern area of the Alliance. Greece has notified NATO that it intends to leave the organisation once again (it left before and rejoined in 1980), although no date has been given and in view of the close ties that exist with other European countries the severence may not occur. In early 1986 the HAF was preparing for delivery of 40 Mirage 2000s and 40 F-16C/D fighters to modernize combat units, the latter type expected from January 1988.

The present front-line force comprises 37 Mirage F.1 interceptors, 53 F-4E Phantoms, 52 A-7H Corsairs, some 60 F-104G Starfighters and 50 ▶

F-5A fighter-bombers, plus six RF-4Es and ten RF-5A reconnaissance aircraft. These are assigned to Wings, or Ptérix, each formed of up to three Squadrons, or Moira.

The Greek national insignia roundel is applied to the wings and fuselage with the vertical markings on the fin. There is no standard type of camouflage on HAF aircraft, the Starfighters and Phantoms retaining the US Vietnam-style two-greens-and-brown scheme while the Mirages have a light blue/grey scheme as delivered. Most of the transports, except VIP and government machines, have a disruptive camouflage.

Serial numbers on HAF aircraft take the form of the machine's construction number or, if the aircraft had a previous identity when it was acquired by the service from another operator, that number retained and painted on the fin. An F-104G, built as 63-12720, went to the Spanish Air Force and was then transferred to the HAF as 32720. This number is carried on the fin with the additional 'buzz' marking FG-720 on the fuselage.

Right: Greece has recieved more than 50 F-104s: this example carries the fin serial 32719 plus the old US-style 'buzz' number FG-719 on the rear fuselage.

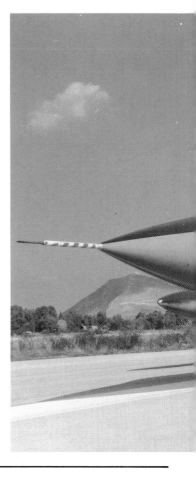

Guatemala

This Central American republic allocates only limited funds for defence purposes and has been unable to add to the eight Cessna A-37B light attack aircraft flying with the single combat squadron. These machines carry the initials FAG (Fuerza Aérea Guatemalteca) on the fin, together with the serial number (three digits ranging between 416

and 460). In addition to the A-37Bs, five PC-7 Turbo-Trainers have been given underwing armament for the attack role and have presumably been camouflaged for the purpose; surviving PC-7s of the 12 originally delivered are retained for use at the pilot training school.

The five-pointed white star on a blue disc is usually painted on the wings and fuselage with the tail marking applied on the fin or, in the case of larger aircraft such as the DC-3 and Arava, as vertical stripes the full width of the rudder in common with other Latin American air forces. Some transports carry FUERZA AEREA GUATEMALTECA along the cabin top.

Guinea

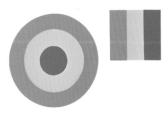

The pan-African colours carried on aircraft of the Force Aérienne de Guinée duplicate those used by Ghana, Togo and the Congo, though in the latter case the design is more elaborate; Mali, Rwanda, and Senegambia also use these colours, though their air arms are too small to warrant inclusion in this book. Confirmation of their application on the eight MiG-17 fighter-bombers supplied by the Soviet Union some years ago has yet to come to light due to the almost total lack of pictures from this country. With the probable poor serviceability of these old aircraft and the small number of supporting Soviet transports (Il-14s, An-14s and Il-18s), it would seem logical for the Guinean Air Force to acquire more modern types such as MiG-21s and An-26 transports, but to date there have been no reports of these types reaching Guinea. Two Romanian-built Pumas are believed to be in service and the only recent acquisition has been a Gulfstream II carrying the civil registration 3X-GBD for VIP use.

Haiti

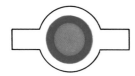

Honduras

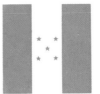

A possible economic revival of a stagnant economy following the deposition from power of Jean-Claude Duvalier in February 1986 may benefit the armed forces of this, the only French-speaking republic in Central America. At present, the Corps d'Aviation d'Haiti has only eight Cessna 337 Super Skymasters converted by Summit Aviation in the US into light attack aircraft with underwing armament points. Four Italian S.211 trainers have recently become the country's first jet-powered aircraft. The national insignia shows strong US influence, reflecting the fact that initial help and equipment came from the USAF. Serials are usually formed of four digits, one of the S.211s carrying 1285 on the fin.

The national marking applied to aircraft of the Fuerza Aérea Hondurena takes one of the five stars from the Honduran flag and locates it between the blue bars, horizontally across the rudder. For the wing marking both roundels and blue-white-blue tips have been used. Israeli Super Mystère B.2s and Arava light transports were acquired in the mid-1970s, but recent aid has come from the US, which has supplied up to 12 A-37B Dragonfly attack aircraft along with helicopters and transports. As with most Latin American air arms, the service initials (FAH) are applied to the fins of most aircraft together with the serial number, which takes the form of three or, in the case of the A-37Bs four digits.

Hungary

Smallest of the Warsaw Pact air arms, the Hungarian Air Force, or Magyar Légierö, has a single air division equipped with fewer than 200 combat aircraft, of which more than half are MiG-21s equipping some six squadrons. Supporting these are three units with nearly 60 MiG-23 interceptors and a small number of MiG-17s, an old but still capable ground-attack aircraft. The national marking on wings and tail of a Soviet star includes the additional green and white colours in the centre to incorporate the Hungarian colours of red, white and green. Aircraft identification numbers, usually formed of three digits, are applied to the aircraft noses in red. Natural metal or camouflage finishes are standard according to role.

India

In terms of numbers of aircraft, the Indian Air Force is judged the world's fourth largest air arm with nearly 900 in service, and since July 1947, when India and Pakistan were established as independent states, it has been engaged in four conflicts. In an effort to provide a modern, effective defensive force, the IAF is in the throes of a major re-equipment programme involving aircraft procurement from both Western and Soviet sources. By 1988 the IAF will be operating MiG-21, MiG-23, Mirage 2000 and Ajeet interceptors and Jaguar, MiG-23BN and MiG-27M tactical support aircraft. It is also expected that the IAF will shortly begin to receive advanced MiG-29 interceptors, probably only after the type enters quantity service with the Soviet Air Force.

The Indian roundel of saffron, white and green is carried on the fuselage, usually on the nose, and on top and bottom surfaces of the wings. The fin flash, with green foremost on both sides, varies in size and position according to aircraft type: some, such as the MiG-23BN, have it near the top of the fin, while ▶

Left: Cruising over a lake somewhere in India, a SEPECAT Jaguar strike aircraft displays the red and yellow chequer marking of 14 Sqn, the first unit in the IAF to attain operational status with the type (in 1980). The aircraft serial is carried on the fin with standard roundels above and below the wings and on each side of the nose.

the Jaguars have a broad marking aligned with the top line of the fuselage. However, in all cases the aircraft serial number is positioned above the marking, usually in black. The number is also carried under the wings.

Indian Air Force serials are allocated in blocks with a role prefix. Three or four numbers form each serial, but for security reasons the IAF leaves groups of numbers out of the blocks, making strength assessment difficult. Even the role prefixes of a particular aircraft type change. As an aid to type identification, some recent prefix letters and representative serials are listed in the table at the foot of the page.

Squadron badges

Squadron badges are applied to some aircraft, usually to the nose or forward fuselage area. Examples are 10 Sqn (MiG-23BNs) carrying a red winged dagger on a yellow disc on the intake sides, 7 Sqn (MiG-21s) with a black battle axe on the nose, 14 Sqn (Jaguars) with red and yellow chequers on the intake side, 37 Sqn (MiG-21s) with a black panther in a white disc, and 5 Sqn (Jaguars) with an elephant on a white or yellow disc on the forward fuselage.

IAF colour schemes are wide-ranging, with some fighter units retaining a natural metal finish for their

MiG-21s, while the attack squadrons have aircraft in different disruptive schemes — green/grey on the Jaguars and at least two different patterns of green/brown/tan on the MiG-23s. Some MiG-21s are sprayed in darker shades of green and grey than those used on the Jaguars, though it would appear from photographs that colours are subject to frequent changes. This is apparent even on aircraft which have been in service no more than a few months, and must be at least partly attributable to the violent extremes of climate to which the aircraft are subject both in flight and when parked in the open on airfields.

Naval Aviation

Aircraft operated by the Navy carry the legend NAVY or INDIAN NAVY and have serials beginning with IN followed by three digits. Sea Harriers of 300 Sqn carry serials from IN601 and a leaping white tiger insignia across the fin as the unit badge; colour scheme of these aircraft is dark grey and white.

Other types in service include Alizé ASW aircraft based aboard the sole aircraft carrier, INS *Vikrant,* and carrying serials in the IN201 range; Islanders; Ilyushin Il-38 patrol aircraft; Kamov Ka-25 ASW helicopters; and Alouette III *Chetak* liaison helicopters.

Indian prefixes and representative serials

B	Sukhoi Su-7BM 'Fitter'	B798-	Approx 140 delivered, all phased out of front-line use
BA	Hawker Hunter F.56	BA201-	Almost replaced by Jaguars
BC	MiG-21F 'Fishbed'	BC820-	Early version, few in service
BH	Hawker Siddely HS.748	BH572-	Used as freighters and trainers
BL	Antonov An-12 'Cub'	BL532-	Being replaced by Il-76
BM	DHC-4 Caribou	BM768-	Due for replacement
C	MiG-21FL/M/MF/bis	C448-	More than 500 delivered
E	Hindustan Ajeet	E1071-	Total of 89 built
IE	Folland Gnat F.1	IE1045-	Most replaced by Ajeet
IF	BAC Canberra B(I).8/PR.57	IF895-	Few remaining mainly for recce
JS	SEPECAT Jaguar	JS101-	Four squadrons planned
JT	SEPECAT Jaguar	JT051-	Two-seat trainers (Jaguar known as *Shemsher* in IAF)
K	Ilyushin Il-76 'Candid'	K2661-	Known as *Gajaraj* in IAF
K	Antonov An-32 'Cline'	K2668-	Known as *Sutlej* in IAF
KF	Dassault Mirage 2000H	KF101-	45 ordered; *Vajra* in IAF service
KT	Dassault Mirage 2000TH	KT201-	Four ordered
SM	MiG-23BN 'Flogger'	SM201-	Ground-support aircraft
U	MiG-21U 'Mongol'	U655-	Two-seat trainer

Indonesia

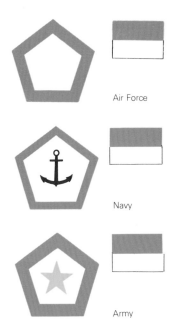

Air Force

Navy

Army

The red and white pentagon marking was adopted for Indonesian military aircraft following the country's achievement of independence from the Netherlands after World War II; the colours are traditional and date back to the 13th century Majapahit Empire. Aircraft operated by the National Armed Forces — Air Force, or Tentara Nasional Indonesia — Angkatan Udara (TNI-AU), carry the marking on wings and fuselage with a red and white flash on the fin.

Only two aircraft types form the front-line combat element of the TNI-AU, the Northrop F-5E and the A-4E Skyhawk. Of the former, 12 were purchased new from the manufacturer, but the 40 or so Skyhawks have been acquired second-hand from Israel and the US Navy. In addition, 16 OV-10F Broncos were delivered for tactical support missions.

Serials are issued in blocks and when applied to aircraft are given prefix letters indicating the machine's specific role. Examples are: TS for fighters, used on the F-5Es (TS-0501-0512); TT for attack aircraft such as the A-4E (TT-0401-); LL for the Hawk advanced trainers (LL-5301-); and HH for helicopters, applied to Bo105Cs (HH-1501-). ▶

Below: Fragile areas toward the rear of the wing are marked with red 'no step' crosses on this Indonesian Hawk.

Indonesian Naval Aviation

GAF Nomads and Searchmasters, Nurtanio-built Bö105Cs and Super Pumas form the bulk of the Tentara Nasional Indonesia — Angatan Laut. Their task is short-range coastal patrol among the country's hundreds of islands to help contain the recent increase in piracy. All TNI-AL aircraft carry the national marking with an anchor symbol in the centre and a prominent serial — usually in black — on the fin. Army aircraft of the TNI-AD (the suffix standing for Angkatan Dorat) are identified by a yellow star in the centre of the red pentagon.

Iran

Operating as the Islamic Republic of Iran Air Force, this former pro-Western air arm is still heavily engaged in a war of attrition with neigbouring Iraq. The equipment used is almost wholly American in origin; despite the lack of spares support from US manufacturers the IRIAF has managed to provide a steady presence over the battlefields for more than six years with the help of spares from 'friendly' countries. .

From pictures and newsreels taken since the overthrow of the Shah, the surviving 40 or so F-4E/D Phantoms, approximately 50 F-5Es and the few flyable F-14 Tomcats appear to have retained the disruptive camouflage schemes applied when the aircraft were delivered. The national insignia also remains the same, but with the addition of the initials IRIAF in place of IIAF previously used. The aircraft serial numbers applied on the fin consist of any combination of up to six digits, although they are allocated in blocks according to type. Phantoms carry numbers in the sequence 3-601, 3-602, 3-603 etc, while Tomcats run from 3-601 to 3-6077.

Unit badges were often painted on the nose or tails of Iranian aircraft, but this practice would seem to have lapsed in recent years, possibly because the shortage of aircraft has necessitated the transfer of machines from one unit to another to maintain strengths at various parts of the battlezone. Transport aircraft (C-130 Hercules, F.27 Friendship, etc) have been seen with Wing badges on the nose, a regular practice back in the 1970s. Both the Army and Navy maintain helicopter forces, in the case of the former mainly composed of Italian-supplied CH-47C Chinooks and AB.205A Iroquois.

Iraq

Dassault Mirage F.1s appear to form the main strike force of the Iraqi Air Force (Al Quwwat al Jawwiya al Iraqiya), with more than 80 ordered or delivered to date. Recent F.1s have replaced five Super Etendards borrowed from France and assigned to the anti-shipping role. Other types in service include MiG-21s, MiG-23s, Su-7s and Su-20s.

The triangular insignia and the fin flash have the same colours as the national flag — red for courage in battle, white for generosity, black for the era of Caliphates and past glory and green for the Islamic prophet Mohammed. Iraqi serial numbers are applied to the fin: older aircraft generally carry three-digit numbers, while later types such as the Mirages and Su-20s are in the ranges of 4000 and 1100 respectively.

Ireland

The Celtic boss marking in its present form was adopted after the Second World War, the three colours from the national flag symbolizing the green countryside and Catholic people along with orange for the Protestants of Ulster in the north and white for the desire for peace between the two communities. It is carried on the wings and fuselage of the nine dark green camouflaged SF.260 Warriors used for training and counter-insurgency duties, the six natural metal CM170 Magisters and the eight green Cessna 172 Rockets. The only other prominent marking is the individual aircraft number, comprising three digits and painted in white on the fuselage of the dark-finished machines and in black on the natural metal aircraft. The current allocations are as shown in the table below.

In addition to the circular national markings, some Alouette IIIs have had large tricolour flags painted on the rear fuselage to clarify the operator during border patrol duties. Dayglo is also carried by training aircraft, usually on the nose, wingtips, tail and around the rear fuselage. Serials are also repeated under the wings.

Irish Air Corps serial numbers

SIAI-Marchetti SF.260WE Warrior	222-235 (nine aircraft)
Potez CM170 Magister	215-220 (six aircraft)
Cessna FR172H/K Rocket	203-243 (eight aircraft)
Aérospatiale Alouette III	195-214 (eight aircraft)
Beechcraft Super King Air 200	232, 234, 240

Israel

One of the most combat-capable air arms in the world, the Israeli Air Force or Heyl Ha'Avir is also one of the most security conscious. Formed in 1948 following the declaration of independence for the State of Israel, this comparatively small force has fought and won three major wars against its Arab neighbours. To the Israelis, one lost war will be the last war.

Israel's national marking is modelled on the Zionist 'shield of David' symbol. On a white background, it has remained prominent on IAF aircraft engaged in front-line and support operations, located on both sides of the fuselage and top and bottom surfaces of both wings. The exception to this practice is the F-16, 75 of which were bought by Israel in the late 1970s to be followed by a further 75 of the improved F-16C version. On these machines, the wing-fuselage blending has meant that no fuselage insignia is carried, national indentification being by means of the 25in (63.5cm) wing markings. To date, all the F-16s noted have employed a disruptive 'sand and stone' camouflage for the attack role (officially designated FS 30219 brown, 33531 yellow and 35622 light blue undersides), as have the surviving 130 or so F-4E Phantoms and the similar number of A-4 Skyhawks, although both types employ green as an additional colour over the top surfaces. The other major combat types are the F-15 Eagle interceptor and the C2 and C7 versions of the indigenously developed Kfir fighter-bomber. ▶

Above: Two F-15 Eagles of the Israel Defence Force/Air Force prepare for take-off.

אלוף-פנקים

Above: 'Skyblazer' in Hebrew on the nose of F-15 No 657 is accompanied by four Arab 'kill' markings. A number of individually marked Eagles equip one of the IAF units.

Right: The F-15s equipping the unit noted above carry the tail insignia seen here, the black and white marking being applied to the inside of the fins. Aircraft 644 is named 'Lightning' while another machine called 'Gunman' sports two 'kills' and has the fin number 678, plus the two Eagle motifs. The counter-shaded greys are shown to good effect in the lower illustration.

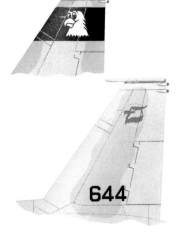

The other official marking applied to IAF aircraft are the individual numbers applied in black on the fin and on the nosewheel door for ground maintenance use. These three-digit numbers bear no relation to the construction number and are not applied in batch sequences, there being numerous gaps intended to confuse enemy intelligence as to the exact IAF operational strength at any given time. For example, the 67 F-16As delivered (incidentally, these were ferried to Israel carrying USAF markings) carry numbers ranging from 100 to 298 and it is quite possible that, periodically, the numbers are changed between aircraft. It is also worth recording that as a further aid to security the same numbers are regularly carried by different aircraft types.

Above: A subtle two-tone grey scheme is carried by this Kfir-C7 fighter-bomber as it taxis out for a mission from a base in the Negev desert. The fuel tanks are still in the old colours.

Right: Tail unit of Kfir-C2 987 in air defence grey. The censoring of tail badges by the Israeli Defence Ministry has been less stringent in recent years, but accurate squadron number tie-ups remain elusive.

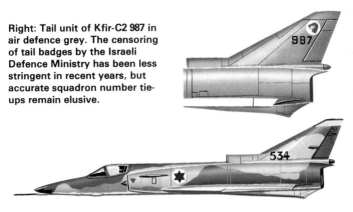

Above: 'Cafe au lait' is the Israeli nickname for this form of desert camouflage evolved for the low- level attack role. IAF fin numbers are known to change, preventing strength assessment.

Israeli Air Force unit badges have been a source of fascination since the 1960s, when the first American equipment joined the squadrons. Any pictures emanating from the IAF or taken by journalists were only released so long as these particular markings were censored. Such was the regular censorship of these badges that some enthusiasts wondered if in fact there were any markings there in the first place. Subsequent investigation and the occasional picture which escaped the sharp eyes of the Israeli press office revealed a range of markings which have appeared in a number of publications, often linked with specific squadron numbers. In the author's opinion, disinformation is still part of Israel's military stance and both numbers and badges remain pure conjecture, and until the restriction on such information is lifted any tie-ups are best treated as unconfirmed speculation.

In addition to the badges, which are usually located near the top of the fin, some aircraft have been seen with red and white or blue and white striped or plain red rudders. Coloured fin flashes (in red) have been noted on Phantoms, a type which has also appeared sporting 'sharks teeth' around the nose. While the IAF has given no publicity to its 'aces' during ▶

recent wars, a number of aircraft have been displayed carrying various miniature Arab roundels on the nose, the highest number to date being 13 applied to the nose of a Mirage III. Eagles have also been shown carrying nicknames in Hebrew, such as 'Gunman' coded 678 with two kills on the nose and cartoon eagles painted on both sides of the vertical fins. Others are 'Skyblazer' with four kills and 'Typhoon' with two kills and the fin number 658.

Among the plethora of markings used on Israeli aircraft, brief mention must be made of the black and orange triangular insignia painted on Mirage and Kfir aircraft in the 1973 war and still seen on some machines. These are used for quick identification and are believed to have been adopted when rumours circulated that Libyan Mirage III and 5 aircraft were to be loaned to the Egyptian Air Force for operations during the war. With Israel already flying these delta-winged fighters, confusion on both

sides would have been a foregone conclusion — hence the IAF decision to paint these panels on their aircraft, including the few Neshers (modified Mirages) used in the war. The Libyan Mirages failed to materialize, but after the conflict, the aircraft flown by the Egyptians also adopted this form of marking.

The civil registration for Israel is 4X, but IAF transports also carry non-military registrations on their wings and fins. The C-130 Hercules range from 4X-FBA to -FBZ, while Boeing 707s flown in the tanker, elint and straight transport roles run from 4X-JYA.

Below: Peace Marble was the code name under which 75 F-16s were delivered to Israel; a further 75 are on order. Aircraft 003, seen here, is a two-seat F-16B and carries 25in (63.5cm) diameter underwing roundels in semi-gloss dark blue and white; US serial was 78-356.

Italy

The Aeronautica Militare Italiano (AMI), or Italian Air Force, assigns most of its front-line strength to NATO's 5th Allied Tactical Air Force for the defence of southern Europe. Of a total strength of some 900 aircraft about one third are combat types, namely Panavia Tornados, Lockheed/Aeritalia F-104G/S Starfighters, and Fiat/Aeritalia G.91Y/Rs; planned for introduction from 1987 are 187 Centauro (AMX) light attack aircraft to replace the G.91s. Basic AMI organization consists of Stormi (Swarms), equivalent to Wings and formed by up to three Gruppi (Groups), each comprising two or three Squadriglie or Squadrons.

The basic AMI marking is the roundel in the national colours. This is positioned in the standard location of wings and fuselage and dates from its use by the Co-belligerent Air Force toward the end of World War II. No tail marking is carried.

Italian military aircraft are allocated serial numbers prefixed MM (Matricola Militare) applied in 10cm-high figures usually toward the rear of the fuselage and above or below the official aircraft designation. Some of the current range of MM serial numbers and their aircraft are given in the accompanying table. The MM serial system is applied to all types of aircraft in blocks according to role as shown.

AMI combat aircraft carry the main formation number (6 in the case of the 6th Stormo) and an individual number. These are applied on the nose or rear fuselage, either split by the roundel or hyphenated. The exceptions to this ruling are some second-line units which have prefix letters followed by the aircraft number. Current combat units can be identified from the table of units and badges (see overleaf).

Some rescue-related helicopters carry disctinctive yellow and red areas plus the abbreviation S.A.R. and the legend AERONAUTICA MILITARE. Navy-operated helicopters can be identified by the word MARINA on the rear boom and an anchor motif, while Army equipment carries the marking ESERCITO and the prefix in the style of E.I. followed by the roundel in most cases and a three-digit number. Finally, mention should be included of the Italian national aerobatic team Frecce Tricolori as one of the most brightly-painted units in the AMI. The MB 339s flown by the unit carry red, white and green colours together with dark blue gloss fuselages and large yellow numbers on the fins. They are a familiar sight at European air shows, and like most national display teams they also have a combat role, as shown by the photograph on page 14-15. ▶

MM serial blocks

MM500	Prototypes
MM5000N	Naval helicopters
MM6000	Jet fighters
MM40000	Atlantic aircraft
MM50000	Trainers and liaison aircraft
MM60000	Transports
MM80000	Helicopters
MM90000	SF.260 trainers

Current Matricola Militare serial numbers

Panavia Tornado	MM7001-MM7090	90 attack versions for AMI
Panavia Tornado	MM55000-MM55009	10 trainers
Lockheed F-104G	MM6501-MM6660	Approx 55 remain in AMI use
Aeritalia F-104S	MM6701-MM6946	More than 110 in AMI use
Aeritalia G.91Y	MM6441-MM6960	About 60 in service
Fiat G.91R	MM6265-MM6424	Due for replacement by AMX
Breguet Atlantic	MM40108-MM40125	18 used for maritime patrol
Lockheed C-130H Hercules	MM61988-MM62001	13 with AMI

AMI combat units, aircraft and badges

2° Stormo	Fiat G.91R	Black lancer over white cloud and blue background
3° Stormo	F-104G	Two black cats' heads and two white cats' heads
4° Stormo	F-104S	White rearing horse on black background
5° Stormo	F-104S	Diana the Hunter drawing bow in white on black background
6° Stormo	Tornado	Red devil's head (Diavolo Rosso) on black background
8° Stormo	Fiat G.91Y	White angel holding a bomb on black background
9° Stormo	F-104S	Black rearing horse on white background
32° Stormo	Fiat G.91Y	Black diving eagle on white background (sharkmouth painted on intake)
36° Stormo	Tornado/F-104S	Silver eagle on white ring and blue background
51° Stormo	F-104S	Black cat chasing three green mice on white backgrounds
53° Stormo	F-104S	Gold and blue scimitar on yellow background
30° Stormo	Atlantic	Purple eagle, white shark, light blue/dark blue background

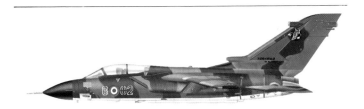

Above: AMI Tornado 6-02 in the markings of the 154° Gruppo of the 6° Stormo. This unit served initially as the Italian AF's weapons training unit; ultimately, all three Italian Tornado Gruppi will be assigned to NATO's 5th Allied Tactical Air Force. The nose code, stencil-split in style, indicates the unit and individual aircraft number. On the fin is the famous red devil badge and below the aircraft name is serial MM7007.

Below: The AMI will receive 100 Tornados, comprising 87 strike versions and 12 two-seat trainers plus a single prototype; this aircraft of the 156° Gruppo of the 36° Stormo is armed with two Kormoran anti-ship missiles. On the fin is the Stormo eagle badge, while the green cat badge of the Gruppo can just be discerned on the engine intake. Roundels are carried on the top and bottom surfaces of the wings as well as on the fuselage.

Ivory Coast

As an ex-French colony, the Ivory Coast adopted a flag with similar dimensions to that of France but formed of orange, white and green. A miniature of this ensign is painted on the fins of the six Alpha Jets in service, the only combat aircraft currently operated by the Force Aérienne de la Côte d'Ivoire. Like other types in use, these machines carry a civil registration in black on the fin (TU-VCA to -VCG); roundels in the national colours are applied on wings and fuselage. Transport, liaison and training aircraft and helicopters have nearly all been supplied by or via France and have military markings plus registrations in the TU-VAA to TU-VZZ block.

Japan

Known as the Sun Disc and originating some 2600 years ago, the Japanese national flag is one of the simplest of designs and is carried on all military aircraft as well as on the aircraft operated by Japan Air Lines. The present design, almost unchanged from those that had gone before, was adopted by the reformed Japanese Air Self-Defence Force (Nihon Koku Jieitai) in 1954. Initial equipment was almost wholly of US origin and with a few exceptions this situation continues today. McDonnell Douglas F-4EJ Phantoms and F-15J Eagles, the latter type replacing the Lockheed F-104J Star-fighters, constitute the major portion of the air defence element protecting the Japanese islands, but these are supplemented by an indigenous design, the Mitsubishi F-1, which is a developed version of the T-2 trainer with only one seat, gun and missile armament and underwing weapon pylons.

JASDF organisation is based on established lines, the largest operational formation being the Air Wing or Kokudan, parent unit to two squadrons or Hikotai; current aircraft holding is officially 18 per squadron although there are plans to increase this to 24. All the JASDF combat units have colourful insignia displayed on the fin. The present JASDF front-line strength is as shown in the table below.

Serial numbers on the aircraft flown by these units are located on the fin, but their composition is somewhat different from the accepted Western form. The six-figure

JASDF combat units

2 Kokudan	203 Hikotai	F-15J Eagle
	302 Hikotai	F-4EJ Phantom
3 Kokudan	3 Hikotai	F-1
	8 Hikotai	F-1
5 Kokudan	202 Hikotai	F-15J Eagle
	301 Hikotai	F-4EJ Phantom
6 Kokudan	303 Hikotai	F-4EJ Phantom
	306 Hikotai	F-4EJ Phantom
7 Kokudan	204 Hikotai	F-15J Eagle
	305 Hikotai	F-4EJ Phantom
8 Kokudan	304 Hikotai	F-4EJ Phantom
	6 Hikotai	F-1

serials are split into a series of individual digits, each of which has a specific meaning. The first digit indicates the year in which the aircraft was purchased; the second is the aircraft type (single- or multi-engined, jet or helicopter); the third is the basic role of the aircraft (see table); and finally the last three form the aircraft's individual, sequential number.

JASDF role numbers

0	Trainers
1	Transports
3	Miscellaneous
4	Helicopters
5	Jet trainers
6	Reconnaissance
7	Day fighters
8	All-weather fighters

An example of the current system, which is used on all JASDF aircraft, is provided by the F-4EJ Phantom serial 57-8359:

Serial 57-8359

5	Aircraft purchased in 1975
7	Jet-powered
8	All-weather fighter
359	The 59th F-4EJ purchased, the first having been given the number 301; a total of 140 were eventually procured

The individual aircraft number is usually repeated on the nose for quick identification purposes on the ground. Maintenance and safety instructions over the airframe are applied in English and Japanese though such instructions do not invariably appear in both languages.

Japanese Maritime Self-Defence Force

The Nihon Kaiyo Jieitai (Japanese Maritime Self-Defence Force) has no pure combat aircraft, but does have an effective collection of ASW aircraft and helicopters. Lockheed P-3C Orions are replacing the turboprop-powered P2V-7 Neptunes for long-range patrol, while Trackers and PS-1 flying boats provide valuable ASW support. Mitsubishi-built Sikorsky HSS-2 Sea Kings are operated from both ships and shore bases.

JMSDF types employ an identification system similar to that of the Air Force, but shorter. The initial figure indicates the type and the other three the individual aircraft number. The key to the present code is as shown.

JMSDF role numbers

2	Single-engined ASW
4	Twin-engined ASW
5	Four-engined ASW
6	Trainers
7	Communications/trainers
8	Helicopters
9	Utility/liaison types

Kawasaki-built P-3C Orion 5015 carries the initial number indicating a four-engined ASW aircraft and subsequent figures denoting the 15th machine of its type in JMSDF ▶

Japan is acquiring 155 F-15J Eagle interceptors including some two-seat F-15DJs. The main view shows an aircraft of the 203rd Hikotai based at Chitose; the scrap view is of the 202nd Hikotai badge.

Frog badge of the 301st Hikotai when it operated F-4EJs from Nyutabaru. The unit will re-equip with F-15Js.

The distinctive flying eagle insignia of the 302 Hikotai, based at Chitose but moving to Naha on Okinawa replacing F-104Js.

Planned to retain the F-4EJ for the near future is the 303rd Hikotai flying from Komatsu under the command of the Central ADF.

Forming part of the defence of south-western Japan is 304 Hikotai, whose Phantoms carry this stylised mask insignia.

Due to receive F-15Js is the 305th Hikotai, but at present (1986) the unit continues to operate F-4EJs from Hyakuri.

The night formation strip is prominent on most of these tails, including this 306th Hikotai example from Komatsu.

Below: Close support is the designed role for the Mitsubishi F-1, hence the three-tone disruptive camouflage which, incidentally, does not wrap around the underside.
This is the first of 77 ordered for the JASDF, the type equipping Nos 3, 6 and 8 Hikotai. Unlike some of the Phantoms in use the F-1s have the great majority of their airframe stencilling in Japanese characters rather than in English.

service. The aircraft number is repeated on the nose. Unit badges are carried on the fins of most fixed-wing aircraft and the title of the operating arm is painte don the rear fuselage of all types in Japanese characters.

Japanese Ground Self-Defence Force

The Japanese Ground Self-Defence Force (Nihon Rikujyo Jieitai) is principally a support force for the ground armies, of which there are five stationed across the Japanese islands. Only Bell AH-1J HueyCobras have an offensive support capability among the types in use, these being armed with cannon and TOW missiles. JGSDF aircraft carry five-number serials, of which the last four digits are normally displayed large on the fin; the full serial is often marked near the nose. The initial digit indicates the machine's primary role and the last four identify the individual machine of the series.

JGSDF role numbers

1	Fixed-wing liaison/observation
2	Fixed-wing miscellaneous
3	Observation helicopters
4	Light transport helicopters
5	Medium transport helicopters
6	Basic trainers
7	Tactical support helicopters
8	Primary trainers

Arm of Service is indicated in Japanese characters on each side of the fuselage, and serial numbers are prefixed JG.

Jordan

Dassault-Breguet Mirage F.1EJ/CJs and Northrop F-5Es form the defensive front-line force in the Royal Jordanian Air Force (Al Quwwat al Jawwiya al Malakiya al Urduniya). Some older F-5As are likely to be disposed of shortly, while 24 Bell AH-1 Hueycobras will soon give the air arm its first helicopter gunships. The national roundel incorporates the seven-pointed star representing the first seven verses of the Koran which form the basis of the Muslim faith, while the fin flash has the same colours as the roundel with the white star on red leading on each side. Individual aircraft numbers are applied on the fuselage sides in Arabic style, although C-130 Hercules transports carry standard

Western numerals both on the nose and fin. The Hercules also have the title ROYAL JORDANIAN AIR FORCE behind the cockpit and one machine (No 347) had 'GUTS AIRLINE' applied on the lower front

Kenya

Known as the '82 Air Force following an attempted coup by Kenya Air Force officers in 1982, the air arm is under the control of the Army but the

national insignia is retained, as is the fin flash. Air defence is the responsibility of a squadron of Northrop F-5Es, ground-attack duties are handled by a unit with BAC Strikemasters, and BAe Hawk Mk 52s are used for advanced training with a secondary attack role.

Aircraft serials are carried on the fuselage with the last two numbers applied large at the top of the fin. Up to four digits are used, with blocks allocated as shown.

Korea (North)

Established in 1948 as a socialist country, the Democratic People's Republic of Korea exists behind almost closed borders, releasing little information about its armed forces. The Korean People's Army Air Force operates aircraft obtained from the Soviet Union and China: from the

fuselage. The civil registration prefix JY followed by another three letters is carried on the Bulldog trainers operated by the RJAF's Air Academy at the King Abdullah base, Amman.

Above: Jordan is one of more than 30 countries to operate the Northrop F-5. This F-5E has the serial number on the fin and miniaturized national markings wings and intakes.

Kenya Air Force serial blocks

100	Light transports (Dornier Do28D-2 Skyservant)
200	Transports (DHC Caribou and Buffalo)
300	Liaison aircraft
400	Transport helicopters (Aérospatiale Puma)
500	Light helicopters (Hughes 500M Scout/500MD Defender)
600	Light attack jets (BAC Strikemaster Mk 87)
700	Trainers (Scottish Aviation Bulldog 103/127)
800	Not allocated
900	Fighters (Northrop F-5E/F)
1000	Jet trainers (BAe Hawk Mk 52)

Aircraft operated by the para-military Kenya Police Air Wing from its base at Nairobi-Wilson are mainly single or twin-engined light machines which carry civil registrations prefixed 5Y.

former, more than 30 MiG-23s have recently been ferried to the KPAAF to join 12 squadrons of MiG-21s in the interceptor role, while from the latter source a number of A-5 attack aircraft have been supplied to add to some ten squadrons equipped with MiG-17s and MiG-19/F-6s. The only light bomber element comprises some 80 obsolete Il-28s.

North Korean aircraft carry the national roundel on wings and fuselage and have individual numbers marked prominently on noses, engine cowlings or nacelles. MiG-21s have carried three-digit numbers in the 200 series, while Antonov An-24 transports have been noted in the 500 and Ilyushin Il-14s in the 700 series.

Korea (South)

Occupying the southern part of the Korean peninsula up to the 38th parallel, the Republic of Korea is supported by the United States in a shaky truce with its North Korean neighbour. The Republic of Korea Air Force (ROKAF), or Han-guk Kong Goon, is almost totally equipped with aircraft of US origin and even the fledgling aircraft industry set up in the late 1970s produces American designs. To bolster the ROKAF fighter units, 36 F-16s are on order to join more than 200 F-5A/Es and 70 F-4 Phantoms.

The Korean national marking is an adaptation of the Japanese rising sun into which blue has been incorporated, divided by a white line and with bars for practical identification.

The abbreviation ROKAF is carried on most combat aircraft and individual machines are identified by the last three digits of the serial number. These are displayed in a larger size on the fin and also on the nosewheel door of the Phantoms in service, if not the other types. Unit bagdes are not displayed for security reasons, the only other markings being the safety and maintenance stencilling which is in both English and Korean. Camouflage employed on the F-5s and Phantoms is the standard US SE Asia two-greens-and-a-brown disruptive scheme.

Photographs of the first F-16D for South Korea, released in the spring of 1986, showed the aircraft in a three-tone grey camouflage scheme with the letters ROKAF and the serial 84-370 on the fin in a shade approximating to the Middle Grey of the radome. A low-visibility version of the national insignia was carried on the wings and aft fuselage, and rescue and maintenance stencilling was also in low-visibility form, again apparently in Middle Grey.

Kuwait

The oil fields and other potential targets of this Middle Eastern country are protected by an air arm equipped with two squadrons of Mirage F.1CK interceptors, backed up by two attack squadrons of A-4KU Skyhawks. Al Quwwat al Jawwiya al Kuwaitiya is a relatively small force

which now relies on these two aircraft types having retired its Lightning fleet: BAe Hawk trainers are replacing the Strikemasters, but reports of Kuwaiti interest in buying up to 20 Panavia Tornados had not been followed up by any order for the type by mid-1986. Desert camouflage is carried by all front-line types (Sand, Light Brown and Grey on the Hawks) and a three-digit serial on the nose in standard figures and on the tail in Arabic script (see the entry on Egypt for Arabic numerals) forms the identifying mark on each aircraft. Examples are given in the table below.

Kuwait Air Force serial numbers

110, 111 etc	BAC Strikemaster Mk 83
140, 141 etc	BAe Hawk Mk 64
501, 502 etc	Aérspatiale SA.342K Gazelle
551, 552 etc	Aérospatiale SA.330F Puma
701, 702 etc	Dassault-Breguet Mirage F.1CK
801, 802 etc	McDonnell Douglas A-4KU Skyhawk

Laos

Equipment obtained from Western sources prior to the 1975 Communist take-over and subsequently with

Soviet aid forms the inventory of the Lao People's Liberation Army Air Force. The interceptor element operates MiG-21s whose exact number and model is unconfirmed, though some sources state 20 MF variants. Markings information too is scarce with photographic evidence of current insignia almost non-existent. National markings are presumed to be carried on the wings and fuselage/tail.

Lebanon

The Lebanese civil war has taken its toll of the country's national air arm, the Force Aérienne Libanaise, particularly with regard to the combat

element of Hunters and Mirage IIIs. Some of the Hunters operated in 1983 at the height of the conflict, but their subsequent fate is unclear, though at least three were lost, while the Mirages had been placed in storage some years ago and probably remain there. Markings were applied in the standard positions and aircraft carried three-number codes prefixed or suffixed with the letter L. The serial on the port side was normally applied in Arabic figures.

Libya

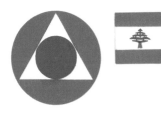

The plain green marking carried on aircraft of Al Quwwat al Jawwiya al Arabiya al Libyya has become a familiar emblem to US Navy aircrew in re- ▶

Below: Mirage F.1ED photographed by a US Navy aircraft off the coast of Libya.

cent years. Apart from shooting down two Sukhoi Su-22s in 1981, USN Tomcats have established regular patrols over the Gulf of Sirte resulting in constant attention from Libyan Air Force Mirage F.1s, MiG-23s and MiG-25s, though not on such volatile terms as before. On paper the LAF is impressive, with more than 500 combat aircraft in service, but its true status and operational capability is considerably reduced from that figure. Aircrew are Soviet, Syrian, Pakistani, North Korean and Palestinian.

The green insignia was adopted following Libya's protest at the visit by President Sadat of Egypt to Israel in 1977, replacing the red, white and black colours that Libya previously shared with Egypt. Aircraft are identified individually by numbers displayed on the fin and nose, sometimes in Arabic form on one side and in conventional form on the other. Three or four digits are usually involved, sometimes reflecting the aircraft serial number as in the case of the Mirages, but no unit badges or other markings are carried. Unusually, some MiG-25s carry two sets of numbers, one example having 499 on fins and intakes plus 1035 displayed either side of the nose.

Malagasy Republic

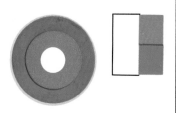

Adopted in 1959, the national flag's three colours signify sovereignty (red), purity (white) and hope (green), the insignia being applied to the fins of the MiG-21s equipping the island's sole fighter squadron. The air arm is known as l'Armée de l'Air Malgache, signifying its previous French connections. Non-combat types carry a civil registration with the prefix 5R-.

Malaysia

The attractive 14-point yellow sun in Malaysia's national insignia represents the 13 states plus the capital territory Kuala Lumpur which constitute the federation. Applied until recently within a blue square; this marking is becoming more common in miniature roundel style on wings and fuselage of aircraft flown by the Royal Malaysian Air Force, or Tentera Udara Diraja Malaysia. The difficult task of defending the country, particularly the capital city, is assigned to a single squadron of Northrop F-5E fighters based in the north

near the border with Thailand. These aircraft remain uncamouflaged with identification serials displayed on the fin in the sequence M29-01, M29-02, M29-03 etc, and like many RMAF aircraft they carry the abbreviation TUDM above the serial. Four F-5F two-seat trainers are serialled M29-15 to M29-18. Note that the RMAF reserialled their aircraft in the early 1980s; the previous style was an FM (Federation of Malaysia) prefix followed by a four-digit number, but by 1986 most aircraft had changed to the new system.

Malaysia has purchased 40 refurbished A-4C and A-4L Skyhawks from US Navy stocks and these aircraft have been redesignated A-4PTM (Peculiar To Malaysia). The 36 single-seaters and four two-seaters equip two squadrons and have a disruptive green and brown camouflage with serials beginning M32-01, M32-02, M32-03 and so on.

Other types in service include C-130H Hercules transports serialled M30-01 etc, plus three patrol versions which carry the legend MARITIM on the fuselage sides; DHC-4 Caribou (M21-01 etc); S-61A Nuri (M23); Alouette III (M20); PC-7 Turbo Trainer (M33); and MB-339A (M34). Most markings are in English, but some stencilling is displayed in Bahasa Malay such as BAHAYA (Danger) and JANGAN TARK ATAU TOLAK (Do not pull or push).

Below: One of 34 ex-US Navy A-4L Skyhawks refurbished by Grumman for the Malaysian Air Force seen in landing configuration. Markings, insignia and stencilling are minimal, with even the widely used red ejection seat triangle missing from under the cockpit.

Mauritania

The national marking of this West African country reflects the Muslim religion of its people. A poor economy has prevented any major expansion of the armed forces despite their being embroiled in a war with the Polisario guerrilla movement. The Force Aérienne Islamique de Mauritanie is principally a transport force equipped with C-47 Dakotas, DHC-5 Buffalos and Short Skyvans, while border patrols are flown by armed B-N Defenders and Surveillance Cheyenne IIs. Almost all FAIM aircraft carry civil registrations within the block 5T-MAA to -MZZ reserved for military machines; commercial aircraft run from 5T-CAA. The national marking is carried on wings and fuselage in the proportion of 3 to 2.

Mexico

The triangular marking applied to aircraft of the Fuerza Aérea Mexicana was first adopted in 1925 and comprises the national colours symbolizing hope (green), peace (white) and unity (red). Applied to wings and fuselage, it is supplemented by rudder stripes in the three colours. The only dedicated front-line combat aircraft in FAM service is the Northrop F-5E/F, 12 of which were ordered in 1981; serials are 4001 to 4010 plus 4501 and 4502 for the two F-5F trainers, and a single squadron operates these aircraft together with a few armed T-33s. More than 50 PC-7 Turbo Trainers are operated in the light attack role, replacing T-28 Trojans and T-6 Texans in a number of units. FAM serials are assigned in four- or five-digit blocks often

Mongolia

The single squadron of Soviet-supplied MiG-21s flown by the People's Army Air Force is one of the least-photographed units in the world. The aircraft arrived a few years ago, replacing MiG-17s in the fighter role, and it can be presumed that the machines carry four- or five-digit numbers on the nose with national insignia on wings and fin. Antonov An-2 biplanes and An-24 transports are also in service. The air force is controlled by the Army and organized along similar lines to that of the Soviet Union.

Morocco

The war in the Western Sahara against the Polisario guerrilla movement has had a deleterious effect on the Moroccan economy, but King Hassan remains determined never to concede the disputed territory. This has resulted in a steady arms buying programme which has seen the influx of military aircraft and ground forces equipment from a variety of countries to maintain Morocco's fighting capability. The Royal Moroccan Air Force or Al Quwwat al Jawiya al Malakiya Marakishiya has received 50 Dassault-Breguet

Mexican Air Force role prefixes

AP	Avión Presidencial
BR	Búsqueda y Rescate (Search and Rescue)
BRE	Búsqueda, Reconocimento y Escuela (Search, Reconnaissance and Training)
EAP	Entrenador Avanzado Pilatus (PC-7 advanced trainers)
EBA	Entrenador Beechcraft Avanzado (Beech Bonanza Advanced Trainers)
EBP	Entrenador Beechcraft Primario (Beech Musketeer primary trainers)
ETL	Escuadron de Transporte Ligero (Light Transport Squadron)
ETM	Escuadron de Transporte Mediano (Medium Transport Squadron)
ETP	Escuadron de Transporte Pesado (Heavy Transport Squadron)
HBRB	Helicoptero de Búsqueda y Rescate Bell (applied to Bell 212 rescue helicopters)
JE	Jet Entrenador (Jet Trainer)
JP	Jet de Pelea (Jet Fighter)
TEB/D/P	Transporte Ejecutivo Beechcraft/Douglas/Piper (Executive Transports)
TP	Transport Presidencial (Presidential Transport)

unrelated to manfuacturers' construction numbers. Normally applied on the aircraft fin, the number is usually prefixed by one or more letters. Those most likely to be noted are shown in the table.

Naval aircraft

Mexican Navy aircraft usually carry the legend ARMADA DE MEXICO, an anchor insignia plus the standard national marking. Serial prefixes include HMR for Naval Rescue Helicopter, ME Naval Trainer, MP Naval Patrol (14 Grumman HU-16 Albatross at several bases), MT Naval Transport and MU Naval Utility. As with FAM aircraft, the serial and triangular marking are also applied under the wings.

Mirage F.1s (25 dual-role F.1EH and 25 F.1CH interceptors), plus 24 Northrop F-5E/F fighter-bombers. Both these types operate in disruptive desert camouflage and carry the national markings on wings and fuselage. The tail flash is formed of a pentagram, or Solomon's Seal emblem, on a red background at the top of the rudder in the case of the Mirages, and located centrally on the fin of the F-5s. As part of the US aid package which included the F-5s, six OV-10 Broncos were delivered in 1981, these being ex-US Marine Corps machines. They retained the dark green colouring overall and even the original black serial numbers at the top of the fins.

Following the non-delivery of some Hughes 500 helicopters, the RMorAF accepted a batch of 24 SA.342L Gazelles, half armed with HOT missiles for the anti-armour role and others fitted with GIAT 20mm cannon and rocket pods for anti-guerrilla operations. These machines have a sand and stone camouflage and have a two-letter code on the tail boom. The Italian-built CH-47C Chinook fleet numbers 12 machines: these have a similar finish but incorporate a five-letter code located at the top of the fin.

A common facet of Moroccan markings is the use of both civil registrations and military serials on many RMorAF types, fighters being the exception. However, the presentation of these markings seems to vary between aircraft. Sometimes it is presented as CN-ASG which is a Puma helicopter, on other occasions as CNA-OR, which has been applied to a C-130H Hercules. All the current registrations fall within the CN-AAA to -AZZ block. The discrepancy in style probably indicates different markings information being provided to the various manufacturers by the RMorAF at the time the aircraft were ordered.

Mozambique

This ex-Portuguese colony became a Communist state on independence in 1975 and has received Soviet aid in building up its military strength. The air force, or Forca Aérea de Moçambique, operates MiG-21s, MiG-23s, Mil Mi-25 attack helicopters and some second-line MiG-17s. Markings are carried on wings and fuselage and aircraft are identified by two- or three-digit serial numbers, usually applied on the nose. The national insignia comprises a gun and a hoe within a gearwheel symbolizing the political movement which heralded independence. Civil registrations are prefixed C9.

Netherlands

The Royal Netherlands Air Force forms part of NATO's 2nd Allied Tactical Air Force and as such plays a vital role in the defence of Western Europe. Known in Dutch as Koninklijke Luchtmacht, the RNethAF has a Tactical Air Command which controls all combat units, presently comprising Canadair NF-5As and GD F-16s, but in the future equipped only with the latter. The first F-16 unit, No 322 Sqn, became operational in May 1981 and total orders for the type to date amount to 213.

The national identity marking appears on both sides of the fuselage, above the port wing and below the starboard wing. Unit badges are often applied to both sides of the fin of both the NF-5 and F-16 (see table), with the individual aircraft number carried below. Three- or four-digit numbers are applied and usually reflect the aircraft construction number. The RNethAF also uses a prefixing system with a single letter allocated to a specific aircraft type. The current list is: A Alouette III (Army); B MBB Bo 105 (Army); C F.27 Troopship/Friendship; H Alouette III (Air Force); J F-16; K NF-5.

The current RNethAF front-line organization is based on a number of squadrons, each with a distinctive badge for which the table below provides a quick check list (note that NF-5 squadrons will eventually convert to F-16s).

The great majority of rescue and maintenance markings applied to Dutch combat aircraft are in English, but a limited number are stencilled on the airframe in Dutch, principally emergency instructions around the cockpit area. Recent changes in camouflage on the NF-5s — a move prompted by the RAF's adoption of grey camouflage for its interceptors — have been accompanied by a sig-

Royal Netherlands Air Force squadron badges

306 Sqn	Eagle's head on black/blue circle	F-16A/B
311 Sqn	Black/white eagle on blue circle	F-16A/B
312 Sqn	Crossed swords and red lightning flash in black circle	F-16A/B
313 Sqn	Eagle on white runway in blue circle	NF-5A/B
314 Sqn	Golden centaur in red circle	NF-5A/B
315 Sqn	Yellow lion's head in blue circle	NF-5A/B
316 Sqn	Brown hawk on yellow disc	NF-5A/B
322 Sqn	Red-tailed parrot in white circle	F-16A/B
323 Sqn	Amazon archer in black circle	F-16A/B

nificant reduction in the size of some of the markings and the elimination of some of the bright colours on the fin badges.

The air arm of the Royal Netherlands Navy, the Marine Luchtvaart Dienst, operates Westland Lynx helicopters designated UH-14 or SH-14 depending on the SAR or ASW role, and Lockheed P-3C Orions. Aircraft are allocated three-digit numbers in blocks, the Lynx running from 260 to 283, and the Orions from 300 to 312. KON. MARINE is applied to the rear fuselage of the Orions and the number is carried under the port wing as well as on the fuselage. A base code letter is painted on the fin and standard national markings are carried on fuselage and wings.

Below: RNethAF F-16As of 322 Sqn with two aircraft of 323 Sqn (5th and 6th from camera) flying in echelon formation. Until a few years ago most pilots wore white 'bone-domes', but these could be spotted at considerable distances, compromising the toned-down airframe colours and markings, so dark green has become the standard colour for this type of headwear.

New Zealand

The Royal New Zealand Air Force is an integral part of the country's tri-service defence organization and operates a modest combat element of McDonnell Douglas A-4 Sky-hawks, supported by BAe Strike-master Mk 88s. There are 22 A-4s in service, single and two-seaters, of which ten are ex-Australian Navy A-4G/TA-4G versions. These and the original RNZAF A-4K/TA-4Ks are being updated and modernized with new radar and attack systems.

The colours of the New Zealand national marking reflect British influence and the tail flash is identical to that used on some RAF aircraft. The kiwi in the roundel is applied facing forward on both sides of the fuselage, while the wing marking follows US practice and is on the top of the

Nicaragua

Prior to the civil war in June 1979, the country's air arm was known as the Fuerza Aérea de Nicaragua, but the establishment of a government by the Sandinista National Liberation Front resulted in a renaming to Fuerza Aérea Sandinista. This title is carried in black on the tail booms of all the Soviet-supplied Mil Mi-8 'Hip' and Mil Mi-25 'Hind' attack helicopters as well as the surviving CASA Aviocar transports. Lockheed AT-33s and armed Cessna O-2s remain from the equipment supplied by the USA before 1979, but to date the long-expected arrival of MiG-21s to provide a front-line defensive force has not occurred, although Nicaraguan pilots have undergone training on the type in Cuba. Three-digit serials are the standard form of identifying FAS aircraft, examples being 340 in black on the nose of an Mi-25 and 281 on the nose of an Mi-8. The yellow and black national insignia is now carried on all Nicaraguan military aircraft; it replaces an interim version composed of the letters FAS attached to a red and black device and a red and black fin flash.

Nigeria

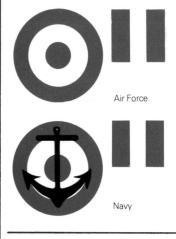

Air Force

Navy

Norway

In a similar manner to some other NATO countries, Norway opted for the GD F-16 to meet her present and future military requirements and, to-day, four of her five front-line combat squadrons are equipped with nearly 70 of these capable fighters. In its present form, the Royal Norweg-

port wing and on the underside of the starboard.

RNZAF aircraft are identified by four-digit numbers prefixed NZ, the A-4s running in a block from NZ6201 with the trainers (TA-4s) from NZ6251, all letters and numbers being in white. The Strikemasters, of which 16 were purchased, have serials from NZ6361 to 6376. To aid identification on the ground, the Skyhawks have the last three numbers repeated in white on the nose. Unit badges of the two squadrons — black and white chequers for 2 Sqn and yellow diamonds for 75 Sqn — are displayed on the engine intakes; the same position applies to the white diamonds forming the 14 Sqn badge on the Strikemasters. Rescue, maintenance and warning stencilling applied to RNZAF aircraft follows standard Western practice.

In early 1986 the Skyhawk fleet carried two different camouflage schemes, the Dark Green/Olive Drab/Light Brown applied to the original K versions and the two-tone grey colours applied by the Australians to the A-4Gs. A standard colour scheme will doubtless emerge when the modernization programme gets under way and the upgraded aircraft are returned to service.

The Nigerian Air Force uses the national green and white colours for its roundel and fin flash. These colours were adopted in 1959, just before Nigeria's independence from Britain, and represent the country's forests with peace and unity. Backbone of the NAF's combat units are the squadrons flying MiG-21MF fighter-bombers, of which about 30 are in service, Jaguars (18 ordered) and Alpha Jets (12 plus 12 on order). All these types are camouflaged, usually in two greens and a light tan scheme on the upper surface and light blue underneath. Each aircraft carries a three-figure identifying serial, prefixed by NAF: the MiGs are in the 650 to 680 range, the Jaguars from 700 and the Alpha Jets from 450, and in almost all cases both numbers and letters are in black. An anomaly was the application of the roundel marking on the fins of the MiGs during the mid-1970s; it is not clear whether this has been changed of late, in line with later aircraft deliveries. MB.339 trainers of the NAF carry the serial on the top of the port wing together with the roundel.

The Nigerian Navy has recently formed a Fleet Air Arm to operate the three Westland Lynx Mk 89 ASW helicopters delivered in May 1984 for service aboard its only major warship, the frigate *Aradu*.

---

ian Air Force, or Kongelige Norske Luftforsvaret, has only existed since 1944 when the Army and Naval Air Services were amalgamated. The RNorAF's delta marking is a postwar design and in line with current NATO practice is being displayed in miniaturized form on the F-16s (and also on the P-3B Orions). Northrop F-5As equip the fifth combat unit and these will remain in service until they are replaced by a further batch of 24 F-16s in 1990-91; the F-5 markings have undergone little change in recent years.

Individual aircraft carry a three-digit identification number on the fin which usually represents the last three figures of the aircraft's construction number. Current examples are: F-16A 272-307; F-16B 658-693; P-3B Orion 576, 583, 599-603; C-130H Hercules 952-957; Sea King Mk 43 060, 062, 066, 068-07, 073, 074 and 189.

Squadron badges are sometimes but not invariably applied to the fins of the F-16s and F-5s. The Sea Kings used for SAR duties have REDNING-STJENESTE along the sides of the cabin, while Coast Guard Lynx helicopters have the legend KYSTVAKT in white on the tail boom.

Oman

Situated on the strategically important Straits of Hormuz — oil gateway to the Arabian Gulf — the Sultanate of Oman has a close affiliation with the Western world and in particular with Great Britain, and with British assistance this moderate Arab country has developed one of the most efficient, if not the largest, air arms in this troubled area.

While future equipment for the combat element of the Sultan of Oman's Air Force (SOAF), or Al Quwwat al Jawwiya al Sultanat Oman, centres on the procurement of an initial eight Tornado fighters, the present strength consists of more than 20 SEPECAT Jaguar International fighter-bombers. Camouflaged in Dark Earth (BS381C-450) and Light Stone (BS381C-361), these aircraft carry serials between 200 and 224 on the rear fuselage in both figures and Arabic script.

The colour scheme wraps round the whole airframe and the only national insignia is a small blue badge with a crossed swords design in the centre. There have been a number of

Pakistan

Air Force

Navy

The five-pointed star and crescent moon of Islam were adopted by the state of Pakistan in 1947 following independence from Britain and the insignia in a green square forms the fin marking on aircraft of the Pakistan Air Force. The wing and fuselage marking consists of a green and white roundel. Early aircraft were obtained from Britain, but Pakistan gradually moved toward the US sphere of influence, acquiring various types during the 1960s from American manufacturers. More recently, 40 GD F-16s have been received to help redress the balance

with the air arms of neighbouring Afghanistan and India. From China, the PAF has purchased 120 Shenyang F-6 fighter-bombers and 42 A-5 attack aircraft, while France has supplied nearly 100 Mirages of various types. More orders are in the offing, probably from China due to the more favourable financial terms.

Individual aircraft numbers take the form of serials based on the construction number. They are carried on the rear fuselage of most types or on the lower part of the fin as in the case of the F-16s. Three- or four-digit serials are standard, often repeated on the nose, sometimes stencil-split or in the angled US style. Some aircraft retain a natural metal finish, notably the F-6s, while others have varying forms of disruptive camouflage such as the A-5s, which are coloured grey/green/buff over the top surfaces and light grey on the undersurfaces. Other schemes include overall light grey and dark green (F-6s) and two-tone grey (F-16s).

The PAF applies squadron badges to the fins of its combat aircraft. Examples are 19 Sqn, which has a green cobra on a white circle on its F-6s; 25 Sqn, which has a black eagle in a yellow triangle on its F-6s; and 14 Sqn, which has a scimitar in a white cirlce on its F-6s. The Combat Com-

different designs and colour combinations for this insignia with some aircraft still carrying the older red and white marking. Apart from the standard rescue and maintenance stencilling, the only other marking is a repeat of the serial number on the nose undercarriage door for ground handling purposes.

Two other front-line types with the SOAF are the Hunter, a batch of 31 having been transferred from Jordan in 1975, and the Strikemaster, which has been operational since 1967. Camouflaged in a new disruptive two-tone grey scheme, these two aircraft conduct ground-attack, patrol and advanced training duties. The Hunters are serialled from 801 onward, while the Strikemasters run from 401 to 424. It is expected that

the Tornados will also adopt the two-tone grey scheme; see page 138 for the Jaguar scheme.

Other types in service include Short Skyvans and B-N Defenders painted in Dark Green and Dark Earth with white over the cockpit area. Three C-130H Hercules are in use together with some helicopters which are operated on SAR duties along the coastal areas of the country.

A Police Air Wing flies a mixture of types on patrol, surveillance and general transport duties around the Sultanate, and each aircraft carries a civil registration of two letters prefixed A40. Examples are Do 228s received in 1984, A40-CQ and CR. All PAW aircraft carry the organization's crest, usually on the fin.

manders School has its initials (CCS) on the fins of its F-6s.

In a similar manner to the fighter units, PAF Hercules transports have mostly been camouflaged in green or brown and light stone colours. The title PAKISTAN AIR FORCE is applied prominently above the forward fuselage and by the cockpit windows is a large single identifying letter, A in the case of C-130B 24141 and S on C-130E 14727, though these letters

Above: Feather-edged green/grey/tan bands form an attractive scheme for these Pakistan-operated Chinese A-5 fighter-bombers. This unit displays its badge on fin and engine intake.

change as aircraft pass through maintenance. The official squadron badge has been seen applied by the forward entry door on the port side. ▶

The air component of the Pakistan Navy has six Westland Sea King Mk 45s serialled 4510 to 4515 and three ex-French Navy Atlantic maritime patrol aircraft. The national insignia has an anchor superimposed and surrounded by a thin yellow line.

An anti-tank capability has recently been conferred on the Pakistan Army with the delivery of 22 Bell AH-1 Cobra helicopters. Other types in use are Puma helicopters from France, Mil Mi-8s from the Soviet Union and home-produced Mushshak (Saab MFI-17) two-seat basic trainers. All carry the title ARMY and the standard national insignia as well as a three- or four-digit serial number.

Paraguay

This land-locked South American country supports three armed services under a unified command. The Fuerza Aérea Paraguaya is mainly a transport and civil aid force with a single combat squadron equipped with the survivors of ten Embraer Xavantes delivered in 1980 as its sole front-line unit. These aircraft carry serials 1001 to 1010 with the last two digits displayed on the nose in black, while national markings are located on wings and fuselage with a small horizontal flash on the fin. Instructional markings on the airframe are in Spanish, including SALVAMENTO for Rescue and PERIGO for Danger, but the marking signs accord with standard Western practice, including such symbols as red/white ejection seat triangles, 'no step' areas and battery location.

Under the current FAP serialling system numbers are allocated as follows: 0001-0999 trainers and liaison; 1000-1999 jets; 2000-2999 twin-engined transports; 3000-3999 miscellaneous types; 4000-4999 four-engined transports.

Peru

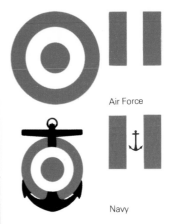

Air Force

Navy

"Look, the flag of liberty!" This exclamation by General Jose de San Martin was prompted by the sight of a large flock of flamingos during this Argentinian patriot's liberation of Peru from the ruling Spanish in 1820. The red and white colours of the birds were adopted for the country's flag, and as a fin flash it is carried by all aircraft operated by the Peruvian Air Force, or Fuerza Aérea Peruana. Roundels are applied in the usual positions on wings and fuselage, but only above the port wing and below the starboard, the opposite locations being reserved for the aircraft serial. Anomalies include Soviet-supplied Sukhoi Su-22 fighter-bombers which carry no fuselage roundels (these and the Antonov An-26s carry a brown and tan camouflage scheme).

Philippines

Bearing a national insignia which closely resembles the American star and bar, the present Philippine Air Force was really only established — with US aid — after World War II. The two main fighter squadrons, the

When Peru received its first Mirage 5Ps, in 1968, it became the first Latin American country to have Mach 2 aircraft in service. Since then more have been purchased and some have received conversions for the anti-shipping role armed with Exocet missiles, and a batch of the latest Mirage 2000 fighters has been ordered. Other combat aircraft in service include various marks of Canberra received between 1957 and 1978, and about 30 small Cessna A-37B light attack aircraft.

FAP aircraft serialling takes a familiar form with the following system: 100 fighters; 200 bombers/fighter-bombers; 300 transports; 400 trainers; 500 miscellaneous types; 600 helicopters; 700 communications types.

Above: Peruvian A-37Bs in standard FAP insignia. This light attack jet was developed from the T-37 trainer.

The FAP appears to leave gaps within some serial blocks which can make assessment of Air Force strength difficult. However, this is not the case with every type in service. Grupo (squadron) badges have been noted on some aircraft and most of the transport and helicopters carry the titles FUERZA AEREA DEL PERU along the fuselage or cabin area. Apart from the tactical camouflages used, FAP rescue and training types employ bright red colours for high visibility, some helicopters being almost totally covered in fluorescent orange.

6th TFS flying Northrop F-5A/Bs and the 7th TFS with F-8H Crusaders, operate in the northern part of the country and form the principal defensive element.

Along with other PAF machines, the two combat types carry the title PHIL AIR FORCE on the nose in the case of the F-5s and along the centre fuselage of the F-8s, while national markings are carried on the fuselage and above the port wing and below the starboard. Individual aircraft are identified by the former USAF/USN serial of which the last three digits

are usually applied larger on the fuselage. The F-8s were given a set of numbers on their delivery which differ from their former USN serials, running from 300 to 324 with another ten held for spares.

With the recent change of government in the Philippines, it remains to be seen whether the activities of the left-wing Mindanao Liberation Front will continue to necessitate the retention of some 30 old T-28 Trojans. These have been operated on COIN duties against the Front for some years and carry the standard in- ▶

signia although some carry no markings at all, being sprayed all-black. Supplementing the T-28s in the attack role have been about 16 Italian SF.260 Warriors. Camouflaged in green and brown with light grey undersurfaces, these machines carry codes from 15-28 to 15-46, the double digits being applied to the fin.

The Air Force is in need of more modern equipment as the F-5s are rapidly ageing and the F-8s are reportedly in constant need of maintenance to keep them flying. Given the recent statement under which the new government has pledged to honour the agreement over the two large US bases in the Philippines, Clark AFB and Subic Bay in Bataan, the PAF may well receive some updated equipment in the near future.

Philippine Naval Aviation has a small support force of Islanders and

Bo105 helicopters. The former carry PHILIPPINE NAVY along the sides of the fuselage and the construction number in white on the fin, together with the large circular arm of service

Poland

As with most of the Warsaw Pact air arms, that of Poland has exhibited no major change in markings for many years, the flair and individuality of western armed forces being almost non-existent in Eastern Europe. Polskie Wojska Lotnicze is the largest of the WP air forces, operating about 900 aircraft, the majority of them MiG-21s, -23s, and -27s, Sukhoi Su-20s and some remaining MiG-17s. All these aircraft carry the red and white national insignia on wings and tail and serialling appears to be in blocks of up to four-digit numbers, sometimes apparently stencilled, and applied to the forward part of the aircraft. Taking the Su-20 as an example of just how difficult it is to assess the number of any type in Polish service, these aircraft have carried numbers ranging from 03 to 04 through to the 6250 range.

Above: 'Hoplite' is the NATO reporting name for the Mil Mi-2 light helicopter which is built under licence in Poland by PZL Swidnik. More than 4,500 have been produced, many for military use, including the Polish Air Force

badge overlapping both fin and rudder.

Note that some government-operated aircraft have serials prefixed RP for Republic of the Philippines.

Above: One of the SF.260WP Warrior COIN aircraft in service with the Philippine Air Force photographed alongside a similarly tasked T-28D.

Portugal

examples seen here armed with unguided rocket packs. Four-digit white serials are applied to the tail booms ranging from 2128 to 3224. On the rear part of the boom is the tail rotor warning sign UWAGA SMIGLO.

The Portuguese Air Force or Forca Aérea Portuguesa uses the Cross of Redemption as the main wing and fuselage marking while the unequal fin flash follows the layout of the national flag with red, representing blood shed, taking more area than the green, meaning hope. Both the Fiat G.91R/T fleet and the Vought A-7 Corsair attack aircraft carry these markings, though in recent years the main insignia has diminished to a less conspicuous size. The majority of the G.91s are ex-Luftwaffe and as such retained their original green-grey camouflage, but this appears to be changing with the apparent adoption of a scheme called NATO South (see photograph overleaf). Serials run between 5442 and 5471 with the two-seaters (G.91T) in the 1800 range; the marking is located at the top of the fin above the flash. ▶

81

Fifty A-7Ps have been acquired for the attack role and these have serials starting from 5501 in sequence. Airframe stencilling is in Portuguese and English, eg RESCUE and SALVAMENTO, DANGER and PERIGO, EJECTION SEAT and CADEIRA EJECTAVEL. The five C-130H Hercules originally received all had US-style Vietnam camouflage with

Below: 'NATO South' is the camouflage scheme now applied to Portuguese Air Force G.91s; 1805 is a G.91T.

serials 6801 to 6805. The Portuguese serialling system follows others, with the first digit indicating the basic type.

Portuguese role numbers

1	Single-engined trainers
2	Twin-engined trainers
3	Liaison aircraft
4	Fighter-bombers
5	Fighters
6	Transports
7	Miscellaneous
8	Staff transports
9	Helicopters

Qatar

The Qatar national flag closely resembles that flown by Bahrain, but the serrated line divides white and maroon instead of red. Miniature presentations of the emblem form part of the tail flash carried on Qatar Emiri Air Force aircraft, while the roundel is displayed in the standard positions on wings and fuselage. The first jets used by the air arm were three single-seat Hunters and a two-seat trainer delivered in 1971. These

carried the serials QA10 to QA13 and flew mainly coastal patrols against smugglers and air defence sorties around the State. Alpha Jets arrived in 1980 for training duties and like the Hunters wore desert camouflage with medium blue undersides and the codes QA50 to QA55.

With many of the surrounding countries now flying much more sophisticated combat aircraft, Qatar decided to invest in a more appropriate defensive force. The result was an order for 12 Mirage F.1EDA fighters and two F.1DDA conversion trainers, their serials being QA71 to QA82 and QA61 and QA62 respectively. Other types in use include Westland Commandos, SA.330J Pumas and three Lynx. Qatar Police Helicopters carry the prefix QP.

Romania

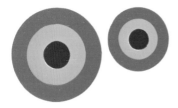

Almost surrounded by other Warsaw Pact members, and sharing one long border with the USSR, Romania carefully maintains itself as a liberalized socialist state within the eastern bloc. The vast majority of the equipment in the Romanian armed forces is of Soviet origin and the air arm is no exception: Fortele Aeriene ale

Republicii Socialiste România has 12 air defence squadrons equipped with MiG-21s and a small number of MiG-23s plus a further six units assigned the attack role with MiG-17s and the first of at least 125 Oraos. Markings incorporating the national colours of blue, yellow and red are applied to the wings and tail of the MiGs, the nose being reserved for the individual aircraft number. Examples are 709, 710, 712, 713 and 714 in black on natural metal finish MiG-21s, 32 and 35 in white on camouflaged Pumas (which are built under licence in Romania by ICA and designated IAR-330), and 706 and 716 on Mil Mi-8 helicopters.

El Salvador

Heavily supported by the United States, the right-wing government in El Salvador continues its guerrilla war against left-wing factions, and to prosecute these operations it has been supplied with a number of COIN aircraft. These are used by the Fuerza Aérea Salvadorena and consist of Cessna A-37 light attack jets, some AC-47 gunships and numerous UH-1 helicopters; they joined an existing front-line force of 18 ex-Israeli Super Mystère B2s, ten Ouragans, eight Fouga Magisters and some

Cessna O-2As for observation duties. Most FAS aircraft carry the national marking in the standard positions with the blue/white/blue flash applied horizontally across the rudder (the colours represent the United Provinces of Central America, adopted in 1912).

The serialling of FAS aircraft appears to follow no logical pattern, some aircraft having a two-digit number while others have three, apparently unrelated to the original construction number of the type. Some examples are the IAI Arava light transports which are 801, 802, and so on, the Ouragans running from 700 to 717 and Cessna T-41s which are 90, 91, etc. Serials are prefixed FAS and some transports, such as the Douglas C-118 301, carry the air force title in large capital letters along the top of the fuselage.

Saudi Arabia

The main feature of the Saudi Arabian national flag is a religious inscription in white on a green field which, translated, means 'There is no God but Allah, and Muhammad is the Prophet of Allah'. Green is the traditional colour of the Fatimid dynasty of Arabia established by Muhammad's daughter Fatima, ▶

chosen because Muhammad reputedly wore a green turban. On aircraft of the Royal Saudi Air Force, or Al Quwwat al Jawwiya al Sa'udiya, a representation of the flag is displayed on each side of the fin (read from right to left). The official title of the air arm is applied in green on almost all equipment and repeated in Arabic immediately above. Serials, too, are marked in both styles.

Replacing the 22 BAC Lightnings operated since the 1960s are 60 F-15 Eagles, uniformly sprayed light grey and forming the country's principal air defence force. Supporting these are some 65 Northrop F-5Es which' are identified by the US military serial, an example being 00918, formerly 73-918. To further expand the RSAF, orders have been placed for 48 Tornado strike aircraft and 24 air defence Tornados plus 30 Hawks and 30 Swiss PC-9 trainers. The first

of the attack Tornados carries the number 701 and a sand, stone and green disruptive camouflage with the standard markings; note that the wing insignia is usually painted above the port wing and below the starboard, the alternative positions being occupied by the initials RSAF in black.

Badges are a feature of some RSAF aircraft, notably the transports of 4 Sqn at Jeddah, which has a full unit badge by the port-side front

Right: No 7 Sqn is the operator of Panavia Tornado 01, the first of 48 strike versions ordered by the Royal Saudi Air Force. It was delivered in March 1986; 24 ADVs are also on order. The roundel marking is applied to the port upper and starboard lower wing positions, with the initials RSAF in the opposing positions.

Singapore

Independent since 1965, the Republic of Singapore initially adopted a conventional red and white roundel for its air arm, but later switched to the present design of two interlocked and stylized fish. This marking is located on the fuselage and wings of the F-5E interceptors and the A-4S Skyhawk attack aircraft operated by the Republic of Singapore Air Force. These two aircraft types are supplemented by about 20 Hunters, the survivors of more than 40 supplied in the early 1970s and the first combat aircraft operated by the RSAF.

Currently, the F-5s have a two-tone light grey finish and carry serials in the 800 range, applied on the fin and nose, while the Skyhawks, sprayed in green and tan camouflage for the low-level attack role, have numbers in the 600 range applied on

the rear fuselage in white with the last two digits displayed on the nose. An example of the latter is No 647, which has 47 on the nose, a Phoenix badge under the cockpit window signifying No 143 'Phoenix' Sqn, and a yellow and black rudder. Other units also have names such as 140 'Osprey', 141 'Merlin', 142 'Gryphon', 120 'Condor' and 130 'Eagle', the badge reflecting the name in each case.

Hercules transports operated by the air arm carry the full title of the force along the forward fuselage,

fuselage entrance door, and 5 Sqn, whose Eagles have a small unit marking on the fin. Instructional and rescue markings over the airframe are often applied in both English and Arabic, the first aid marking taking the form of the Muslim crescent in the place of the red cross.

small representations of the national insignia on fuselage and wings and the three-digit serial on the fin in black, for example 725 and 732, the 25 and 32 being repeated on the nose. In addition to the serials noted above, other types are SF.260MS 120, 121, etc; SF.260W 151, 152, etc; BAC Strikemaster Mk 84 300, 301, etc; SIAI-Marchetti S.211 380, 381, etc; and HS Hunter 500, 501, etc.

Below: Singapore Air Force TA-4S trainer 687. The original US Navy Bureau No 144894 is still carried on the nosewheel door.

Somalia

The national markings of Somalia date from 1954 and the adoption of the white star originally used by the southern part of the country; the Somali Air Force (Dayuuradaha Xoogga Dalka Somaliyeed) took the insignia and formed a roundel which is currently used on wings and fuselage. Previous Soviet influence is manifest in the form of some surviving MiG-17s and -21s, but more recently Somalia turned to the West, and in particular to Italy, her former colonial trustee, for both economic and military aid. The result was the delivery of some SF.260W armed trainers (serialled 60-SBC, -SBD etc), four G.222 transports (AM94-AM97) and some HS Hunters acquired from Kenya and Abu Dhabi. Four ex-Abu Dhabi Islanders are also in use. A leaping tiger in yellow was applied to the nose of the G.222s.

South Africa

Since 1957 aricraft of the South African Air Force have carried the national marking shown above, consisting of a plan of the fort at Cape Town enclosing the springbok symbol. It is located in the standard positions on most aircraft although for service in the 'operational area' it is sometimes deleted from the more prominent positions. The tail stripes represent the national flag and originate from the emblem of the Dutch Prince of Orange, which was brought to the country by the early settlers in the seventeenth century. It is sometimes sprayed over the whole rudder, as on the Mirage F.1s, or as a much smaller oblong on the fins, as on the Harvards still in service. Transports which carry camouflage do not generally use a fin flash.

Government and VIP aircraft such as the single Viscount and the HS.125s display the legend SOUTH AFRICAN AIR FORCE in the case of the former and S.A. AIR FORCE on the latter.

The SAAF is heavily committed to the war along the northwestern border between Namibia and Angola, though in early 1986 this generally involved only relatively light aircraft such as the indigenous Bosbok observation aircraft, the Kudu transport version, and the MB.326 Impala II attack jet. Major targets involve the more powerful Canberra or Mirage III force. Helicopters are the workhorses of the war with Alouette IIIs and Pumas the most widely used.

Of the main combat types in SAAF use, the Mirage F.1CZ fighter and F.1AZ attack version are the most important. The serials applied on the rear fuselage run from 200 to 215 on the former type and 216 to 247 on the latter. Camouflage for the attack version is Olive Drab (BS381C -298) and Deep Buff (360) with Light Admiralty Grey (697) underneath, but there have been recent indications that the fighter CZs are adopting a light grey overall finish in place of the disruptive scheme.

The other Mirage IIIs are of various types, including fighters, trainers and reconnaissance aircraft. Their serials run from 800 to 857 and their camouflage is the same as that applied to the F.1s. Long-range strike is the task of six Buccaneer S.50s remaining of 16 ordered and 32 required but not delivered. Serials are included between 411 and 426, and the colours are Dark Sea Grey (638) on the upper surfaces and PRU-blue (636) underneath. Six Canberras (451 to 456) were delivered in 1963 and are finished in PRU-blue. The Italian-designed single-seat MB.326KC Impala II was built by Atlas Aircraft in South Africa and at least 70 were delivered to the SAAF carrying serials 1001 to 1090. Like most tactical aircraft, they have the last two digits repeated on the nose in black and their camouflage is a scheme of Olive Drab (298), Dark Earth (450) and Light Admiralty Grey (697).

Squadron badges reflect long traditions in the SAAF and are carried by a number of types, usually on the fin but sometimes on the engine intake or under the cockpit. Current examples are as shown.

SAAF squadrons, badges and aircraft

1 Sqn	RAF eagle holding a Crusader's shield	Mirage F.1AZ
2 Sqn	Flying cheetah with motto 'Upward and onward'	Mirage III
3 Sqn	Hornet with motto 'Always fighting'	Mirage F.1CZ
4 Sqn	Bat on blue circle with motto 'Death to the enemy'	Impala II
12 Sqn	Winged springbok — 'First into battle'	Canberra
24 Sqn	Diving eagle on black and white circle — 'Through night, through day'	Buccaneer

The helicopter force of Alouette IIIs, SA.330 Pumas and Super Frelons has a uniform colour scheme consisting of Olive Drab and Dark Earth with two or three digits identifying the individual aircraft. The serial numbers of the Alouettes range from 23 to 637, those of the Pumas from 120 to 186 and those of the Frelons from 301 to 316.

Soviet Union

The Soviet Union operates more aircraft than any of the world's air forces, with the possible exception of that of the United States. Unlike most countries, the Soviet Union has four major combat air arms organized to provide dedicated aviation support where it is needed at the most decisive place and time. The main components are the Strategic Air Armies, Air Forces of Military Districts and Groups of Forces, Military Transport Aviation and the Naval Air Force. Aircraft are stationed throughout the USSR, at bases in the neighbouring Warsaw Pact countries, and overseas in Cuba, Vietnam and on temporary detachment to a number of other friendly nations. ▶

Below: A Soviet Air Force officer poses with ground crew in the cockpit of a MiG-23 fighter. It appears to be a well-used aircraft and it is interesting to note the 'NATO marking' for the hoist point prominently displayed under the cockpit quarter-light. Bort number 99 is red, outlined in black.

Almost all combat aircraft display the distinctive red star of the Communist party on their fins and wings, usually outlined in white or the official yellow as applied to the national flag. The exceptions to this rule involve certain aircraft operated by the transport force which often carry civilian registrations for flights outside the borders of the USSR. Prefixed CCCP- (or in English SSSR-) and usually carrying Aeroflot livery, these aircraft have five-digit numbers, an example being an Antonov An-12 CCCP-11037 seen over the Indian Ocean by US Navy fighters. However, it should be realized that the Soviet air transport fleet of airliners and cargo aircraft becomes part of the military forces in time of war.

Before looking at the various markings used by current Soviet military aircraft, it is as well to list the code names applied to these types by the NATO countries. These are reporting names given to each new type as it is revealed because the closed society in the USSR often prevents the true designation of an aircraft becoming known. The names are allocated by the West's Air Standards Co-ordinating Committee (ASCC) and follow the system of B for bombers, F fighters, C commercial aircraft (airliners and transports), H helicopters and M miscellaneous. As new versions of a particular type are identified they are given suffix letters; the 'Badger', for example, which is the Tupolev Tu-16 bomber, has been given ten suffix letters — A, B, C and so on — identifying the various versions. The present list is correct up to May 1986.

NATO reporting names

Backfire	Tupolev Tu-22M
Badger	Tupolev Tu-16
Beagle	Ilyushin Il-28
Bear	Tupolev Tu-20/142
Bison	Myasischev M-4
Blackjack	Tupolev Tu-?
Blinder	Tupolev Tu-22
Brewer	Yakovlev Yak-28
Fagot	Mikoyan MiG-15
Farmer	Mikoyan MiG-19
Fencer	Sukhoi Su-24
Fiddler	Tupolev Tu-28
Firebar	Yakovlev Yak-28P
Fishbed	Mikoyan MiG-21
Fitter	Sukhoi Su-7/-17/-20/-22
Flagon	Sukhoi Su-15
Flanker	Sukhoi Su-27
Flogger	Mikoyan MiG-23/-27
Forger	Yakovlev Yak-38
Foxbat	Mikoyan MiG-25
Foxhound	Mikoyan MiG-31
Fresco	Mikoyan MiG-17
Frogfoot	Sukhoi Su-25
Fulcrum	Mikoyan MiG-29
Camber	Ilyushin Il-86
Camp	Antonov An-8
Candid	Ilyushin Il-76
Careless	Tupolev Tu-154
Cash	Antonov An-28
Clank	Antonov An-30
Classic	Ilyushin Il-62
Cleat	Tupolev Tu-114
Cline	Antonov An-32
Clobber	Yakovlev Yak-42
Clod	Antonov An-14
Coaler	Antonov An-72

Cock	Antonov An-22
Codling	Yakovlev Yak-40
Coke	Antonov An-24
Colt	Antonov An-2
Condor	Antonov An-124
Cookpot	Tupolev Tu-124
Coot	Ilyushin Il-18
Coot-A	Ilyushin Il-20
Crate	Ilyushin Il-14
Creek	Yakovlev Yak-12
Crusty	Tupolev Tu-134
Cub	Antonov An-12
Curl	Antonov An-26
Halo	Mil Mi-26
Harke	Mil Mi-10
Havoc	Mil Mi-28
Haze	Mil Mi-14
Helix	Kamov Ka-27/-32
Hind	Mil Mi-24/-25
Hip	Mil Mi-8
Hokum	Kamov Ka-?
Hook	Mil Mi-6
Hoplite	Mil Mi-2
Hormone	Kamov Ka-25
Hound	Mil Mi-4
Maestro	Yakovlev Yak-28U
Mail	Beriev Be-12
Mainstay	Illyushin Il-?
Max	Yakovlev Yak-18
May	Ilyushin Il-38
Maya	LET L-29 Delfin
Midas	Ilyushin Il-?
Midget	Mikoyan MiG-15UTI
Mongol	Mikoyan MiG-21U/UM
Moose	Yakovlev Yak-11
Moss	Tupolev Tu-126
Moujik	Sukhoi Su-7U

Strategic bombers (Tu-22Ms, Tu-16s, M-4s and Tu-20/142s) carry hardly any markings apart from the standard national insignia. A large two-digit number used to be applied to the nose and a small duplicate was painted at the top of the fin, but this has now been reduced to the fin number sometimes being retained and a small presentation on each of the nose-wheel doors for identification on the ground. Examples are 55 in red on a Tu-16 reconnaissance aircraft and 15 on a Tu-20 (top of fin and on nosewheel doors). These numbers are unit identification codes and do not reflect 'build' numbers which are seldom seen, although they are applied to some machines. One which was noted was 1880302 on a Tu-16 carrying the large number 50 and another on a Tu-22 5050051 with the main number 32. These long numbers are believed to encompass the factory construction number and possibly the batch, but this is unconfirmed.

Fighter aircraft also carry a two-digit identification in colours which include red, blue and yellow in various styles, but all quite large and prominent. Squadron or regiment badges are never displayed, but to maintain some sort of *esprit de corps*, the operating commands issue unit efficiency awards, the badges of which are allowed to be displayed on the noses of the privileged squadron's aircraft. The most common of these markings, a stylized aircraft over a pentagon shape in red on a metal background

Above: The sheer size of an aircraft like this 'Bear-H' of the Soviet Long-Range Bomber force probably dissuades personnel from applying more than the most basic markings and insigia.

or yellow on painted aircraft, has been seen on bombers, fighters and combat helicopters. A second insignia which has been seen increasingly on Su-17 ground-attack aircraft is a winged marking in blue and white, but much larger than the previous badge; its exact meaning has yet to be confirmed.

Aircraft and helicopters operated by the Naval Air Force can be identified by the naval ensign which is carried by ship-based types, although the long-range element flying Tu-16s, Tu-22Ms, Tu-142s and Il-38s retains the usual Soviet military anonymity. Yak-38 vertical take-off combat aircraft operating from the Kiev class carriers display the standard two-digit numbers (examples are 32, 54 and 50 in yellow outlined in black) on the dark blue top surface colour. One interesting example was No 46 which carried three small naval flag markings under the cockpit while on the rear fuselage was a small 'build' number 7977863822385 in yellow. The complications of using such an unwieldly string of digits can easily be imagined, if indeed these do relate to the factory production line.

Soviet military aircraft are not noted for special markings, though they appear to employ them when necessary, such as during the inva- ▶

sion of Czechoslovakia, when MiG-21s appeared carrying red and yellow bands around the rear fuselage. Air Force aerobatic teams have received colourful schemes similar to those in the West, but generally the Soviet air arms are drab and colourless. Finally, the maintenance and servicing instructions around the airframe of a Soviet military aircraft are relatively few in number, but those that are there are in Russian. However, many of the markings and symbols are identical to those on NATO machines. Is this planning for the future or just a sensible adoption of a practical range of markings?

Above: Soviet aircrew pose for a TASS photographer at an Su-17 'Fitter' base in Russia. Aircraft 05 has a small unit commendation badge in front of the large blue and white number. All the aircraft have intake warning markings in red and black.

Below: Kubinka air base near Moscow is the home for this MiG-23 'Flogger-G' fighter, part of a special demonstration squadron tasked with overseas visits and displays. These aircraft operate without weapons or pylons, although these can be fitted.

Spain

One of NATO's southern members, Spain is integrating its latest combat aircraft into service following receipt of the first of 72 McDonnell Douglas F/A-18 Hornets in mid-1986. These aircraft, like their predecessors over the past 50 years, carry the red and yellow roundel of Aragon, colours which date back to the twelfth century, when they were used by the Kingdom of Aragon. The black diagonal cross on a white background is more recent and only dates from the Spanish Civil War of the late 1930s. The Spanish Air Force, or Ejército del Aire Espanol, has a combat force of some 180 aircraft operating under the auspices of three of the four main commands, Air Combat, Air Tactical and Air

Below: Spain acquired 40 F-4C Phantoms, this being the 23rd; it has the markings of 121 Escuadron on the engine intake. National insignia is small and colours are Vietnam style.

Command of the Canaries; the fourth is Air Transport. Types in service are Mirage F.1CE and Mirage IIIEE interceptors (the latter to be replaced by the Hornets), F-4C/RF-4C Phantom attack/reconnaissance aircraft, and Spanish-built SF-5A ground-attack aircraft. Spanish military aircraft carry individual serial numbers, prefixed by an aircraft code which is allocated to each aircraft type.

Spanish role prefixes

A	Attack
C	Fighter
D	Rescue
E	Trainer
H	Helicopter
P	Patrol
R	Reconnaissance
T	Transport
TK	Transport-tanker
UD	Utility
VA	V/STOL attack
Z	Previously helicopters, replaced by H

An example of the system is an F-4C Phantom which has C12-30 applied in black on the fin, indicating fighter of the 12th type (a Phantom), and the 30th of its type in service. Where aircraft have a dual role or a specialized task a combination of letters is carried, such as CR12 for the ▶

reconnaissance version of the Phantom. Aircraft operating in the Spanish Air Force, Army and Navy carry the basic letter/number designators shown.

Spanish type designations

A9	SF-5A
AE9	SF-5B
AR9	SRF-5A
C11	Mirage IIIEE
CE11	Mirage IIIDE
C12	F-4C Phantom
CR12	RF-4C Phantom
C14	Mirage F.1CE
C15	F/A-18 Hornet
D2	F.27-400MPA Maritime
E14	HA.200 Saeta
E15	Lockheed T-33A
E18	Piper Navajo
E19	Piper Aztec
E20	Beech Baron
E22	Beech King Air
E24	Beech Bonanza
E25	CASA 101 Aviojet
E26	ENAER T.35 Pillan
H7	Bell 47G Sioux
H8	Bell UH-1B/204
H9	SH-3D/G Sea King
H10	Bell UH-1H
H12	Bell OH-58A/206
H13	Hughes 500M
H14	Bell AH-1G Cobra
H15	MBB Bö 105C
H16	Alouette III
H17	CH-47 Chinook
H18	Agusta-Bell AB-212ASW
H19	SA.330 Puma
H20	Hughes 269
H21	AS.332 Super Puma
H22	MBB BK117
P3	P-3A/B Orion
T3	Douglas C-47
T9	DHC-4 Caribou
T10	C-130H Hercules
TK10	KC-130H Hercules
T11	Falcon 20
T12	CASA 212 Aviocar
U9	Dornier Do 27
UD13	Canadair CL-215
VA1	AV-8A Matador

Right: Spanish Navy AV-8A Matador of 008 Escuadrilla displaying the naval wings on the fin and the prominent MARINA on the rear fuselage. Although built in the UK, these machines were officially supplied by the USA and have Bureau Numbers.

In addition to this system, Spanish aircraft also have a unit coding which indicates the Escuadron (squadron) and the individual machine in that unit. To take Phantom C12-30 again, this aircraft carries the number 122-15 in black on the engine intakes, 122 indicating Squadron 122 and 15 being the machine's unit number. Sometimes the national roundel on the fuselage divides the unit code and aircraft number. Up to four squadrons make up a group or wing (Ala), though the normal complement is two, and each of the squadrons wears the wing badge, the main ones being:

Fighter wing 11 (two squadrons of Mirage IIIs): Three diving birds in blue on a white disc.

Fighter wing 12 (two squadrons of Phantoms): Dark blue wildcat's head.

Fighter wing 14 (two squadrons of Mirage F.1s): Don Quixote with three Mirages and No 14 in red.
Attack wing 21 (one squadron of SF-5s): Blue and white shield with black F-5 silhouette.
Wing 46, in the Canaries (one squadron of Mirage F.1s): Black 46 on red circle.

Naval aircraft
Spanish Naval aircraft bear the legend MARINA on the rear fuselage of the AV-8 Matadors and on the tail boom of the helicopters. Wing markings for the Matadors consist of standard roundels in addition to the individual aircraft number and unit on the upper surface of the port wing and the word MARINA with roundel above the starboard side. A winged anchor symbol is carried by all naval-operated machines.

Sri Lanka

Independent from Britain since 1948, Sri Lanka was formerly named Ceylon and its air arm, the Sri Lanka Air Force, has an insignia formed from the main elements of the national flag. The green and orange in the bars represent the Muslims and Hindu Tamils respectively, while the maroon and yellow are the colours of the old flag of Kandy, the ancient kingdom in the centre of the island. The country's brief association with the Soviet Union resulted in the delivery of a handful of MiG-17s, but these have long been out of service. Transport and liaison duties are the main tasks of this small force which has a collection of helicopters and fixed-wing types for both civil and military use.

Serials consist of a prefix letter C for Ceylon and a role letter: A for advanced trainers, C single-engined transports, F fighters, H helicopters, J jet aircraft, R multi-engined transports, S surveillance aircraft and T trainers. Thus CH-531 and -532 are SA.365C Dauphins; CC-650 and -651 are Cessna 337s; CR-841 is a Super King Air; and CR-801 and -802 are DH Herons.

Sweden

The Kingdom of Sweden maintains a large air force to protect its neutrality in a Europe divided by two markedly different ideological systems into the two armed camps of NATO and the ▶

Warsaw Pact. Her borders are with Norway in the west, fellow neutral Finland in the north and, across the Baltic in the east, with the Soviet Union. To reduce the reliance on outside arms suppliers, Sweden has developed an industrial base which has designed and produced the past and present military equipment of all three services and is currently working on the country's future needs to continue doing so into the twenty-first century. The Royal Swedish Air Force (Flygvapnet) has an interceptor force of some 200 aircraft divided between new JA 37 Viggens and older J 35 Drakens, both products of Saab. For the 1990s, the Air Force will receive a planned 140 JAS 39 Gripen to replace the Viggen fleet, variants of which are also in use in the attack and reconnaissance roles.

The Swedish national marking bears the colours of the flag but incorporates the three crowns derived from the ancient state coat-of-arms dating from 1364. The insignia is carried on the forward fuselage and wings of all Sweden's combat aircraft. Two other prominent markings are located on each aircraft: on the nose is the number of the Flottilj (wing) to which the aircraft belongs, and on the tail is a two-digit number allocated sequentially through the two combat squadrons which currently form a wing.

On the attack and reconnaissance Viggens, the tail code is applied in dayglo orange over the complicated splinter camouflage pattern adopted in the 1970s. This consists of black green, mid-green, light green and stone with light grey on the under-surfaces. Fighter versions of this capable canard design have recently acquired a light grey low-visibility finish in accord with other air forces in Europe. Serial numbers on the combat types are applied in 3in (76mm) figures on the rear fuselage, in yellow on camouflage and black on natural metal finishes, and consist of five digits, those on the Drakens running from 35000 and those on the Viggens from 37000.

Military aircraft in Sweden are given different designations from those operated by other countries. Each type has a role prefix letter followed by a sequential number. While the number remains the same, an aircraft having a change of role will also have a change of prefix. The current list is: A Anfallplan (attack); Hkp Helikopter; J Jaktplan (fighter); S Spanplan (reconnaissance); Sk Skolplan (trainer); Tp Transportplan. Swedish military aircraft and their designations are as shown.

RSAF aircraft designations

Hkp 2	Alouette II
Hkp 3	Agusta-Bell AB.204B
Hkp 4	Vertol 107-II
Hkp 5	Hughes 300
Hkp 6	Agusta-Bell AB.206A
J 32	Saab Lansen
J 35	Saab Draken
J 37	Saab Viggen
Sk 50	Saab 91 Safir
Sk 60	Saab 105
Sk 61	Scottish Aviation Bulldog
Tp 79	Douglas C-47
Tp 84	Lockheed C-130 Hercules
Tp 85	Caravelle III
Tp 86	Rockwell Sabreliner
Tp 87	Cessna 404
Tp 88	Swearingen Metro

The Viggen has been produced in five different versions: the AJ 37 attack aircraft, JA 37 fighter, SF 37 reconnaissance, Sk 37 trainer and SH 37 maritime surveillance aircraft.

Stencilling and maintenance instructions are applied in Swedish, ▶

Above: Without doubt one of the most complex comouflage schemes ever applied to a production aircraft, this four-colour pattern has been applied to Swedish Viggens since the early 1970s. This AJ 37 attack version carries the nose code of F13 Wing and, coincidentally, the individual aircraft number 13 on the fin below the unit badge.

Left: In plan, the prominent wing insignia contrast strongly against the Viggen's disruptive colour scheme. An impending attack on Sweden would prompt the dispersal of the Flygvapnet fleet to prearranged locations on the country's road system where prepositioned fuel and ammunition would sustain it.

the most obvious being FARA (Danger) painted on the engine intakes. Also note that the fin code number is repeated in black on the Viggens' main undercarriage doors. For tactical exercises, Drakens have large white numbers applied to their wings, the overall proportions being 250cm (98½ in) in height and 120cm (47¼ in) in width.

Above: The angled undernose indicates a photoreconnaissance S 35E Dracken. Few of these remain in RSAF service, their role being taken over by the SH/SF 37 Viggen: F16 at Angelholm and F15 at Uppsala are now the only Draken Wings and only the former is likely to retain the type.

Switzerland

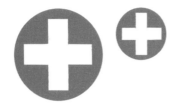

A feature of Switzerland's neutrality is the country's preparedness for war. Stretches of roadway are specially designated as runways, mountains have huge caverns buried in them to accommodate whole squadrons of aircraft and their supplies, and almost all Swiss citizens are members of either the full-time military or the part-time militia. The Swiss Air Force, or Flugwaffe, is a branch of the Army and its first role is to detect, identify and react to foreign air incursions from any direc-

tion, while its second task is to support the ground troops and provide them with a protective air umbrella. The three types of combat aircraft in service, totalling some 260 aircraft, are Hawker Hunters, Northrop F-5Es and Dassault-Breguet Mirage IIIs. The main insignia is identical to that on the Swiss flag and is applied in the standard wing positions and on the fin on all military aircraft. The fuselage is reserved in most cases for the identification number, of four digits in the case of the front-line machines and of three on support types.

Using a style similar to that employed by other air arms, the Swiss serialling prefix system has an identifying role letter: A for Anfänger (learner, or trainer); C Utility; J Jägd (hunter, or fighter); R Reconnaissance; U Übungsflugzeug (practice aircraft, or trainer); V Verbindungs

(communications). Aircraft operated by the Swiss Air Force can therefore be readily identified as to their role. Some of the current types and their serial ranges are listed in the accompanying table.

Above: The second of six Northrop F-5F trainers (J-3201 to J-3206) originally delivered to the Swiss Air Force. A further six were subsequently received ▶ under US Peace Alps contracts.

Swiss Air Force serial numbers

Beech Twin Bonanza	A-711 to A-713
Pilatus P-3	A-801 to A-873
Pilatus PC-7	A-902 to A-941
EKW C-3605	C-400/500 range
de Havilland Vampire FB.6	J-1000 range
Dassault-Breguet Mirage IIIS	J-2301 to J-2336
Northrop F-5E/F	J-3001 to J-3207 +
Hawker Hunter F.58/T.68	J-4001 to J-4208
Dassault-Breguet Mirage IIIRS	R-2101 to R-2118
Pilatus P-2	U-101 to U-157
de Havilland Vampire T.55	U-1201 to U-1239
Dassault-Breguet Mirage IIIBS	U-2001 range
Sud Alouette III	V-201 to V-284
Dornier Do 27	V-601 to V-607
Pilatus PC-6 Porter	V-612 to V-635

Not all the aircraft listed will be operational, and gaps occur in the batches, but it will give an idea of the composition of types within the air arm. The wide dispersal of units around the country and the natural security cloak surrounding unit locations make squadron/code/base tie-ups difficult, but the basic formation is the squadron, with up to eight squadrons forming an Air Regiment.

Additional markings involve the application of the last three digits of the serial on the nose of the aircraft, as seen on the F-5s, while some of the Hunters have only the last two digits on the nose and on the nosewheel door. Maintenance markings are normally applied in French and German. Unit emblems are car-

ried on only two or three aircraft in each squadron but they serve to identify the unit. Examples are 17 Sqn (Mirages) which has a red diving bird on a white circle, 11 Sqn (F-5Es)

Right: One of the 98 F-5E Tiger IIs bought by the Swiss and an integral part of the country's defenses. The subtle difference between the two shades of grey can be seen on the wings.

Syria

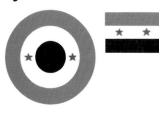

Supported and supplied with military aircraft and equipment by the Soviet Union, Syria has fared badly when flying in combat against Israel, despite having some of the most capable front-line types in service. The Syrian Arab Air Force is known as Al Quwwat al Jawwiya al Arabiya as'Souriya and operates MiG-21s, MiG-23s and MiG-25s in some 15 fighter squadrons. These machines carry the national marking shown above in the standard positions and have individual numbers, usually based on their construction numbers, located on the nose in Arabic characters. The tail flash is a repeat of the national flag and it is also applied to aircraft operated by the airline SyrianAir.

Above: To most people it is an F-5E, but to the Republic of China Air Force it is the Chung Cheng and 256 are being built in Taiwan to infuse some

with a yellow tiger's head on a black circle, 10 Sqn (Mirage IIIRS) with a red/white bird's head in arrow style, and a black panther on a green shield on 18 Sqn Hunters.

Taiwan

In 1928 the Nationalist party in China adopted a new flag with a 12-pointed star, each point representing the two-hour period of the Chinese day. When the Nationalist forces of General Chiang Kai-shek were defeated by the Communist army of Mao Tse-tung in 1949, the survivors moved to the island of Formosa and set up the state of Nationalist China. Now called Taiwan, this state has established its own industry to supply the armed forces with helicopters (118 licence-built Bell UH-1H for the Army), jet trainers (more than 50 AT-3s on order for the Air Force) and tactical fighters. The last-mentioned are licence-built Northrop F-5Es, 256 having been produced under the name Chung Cheng along with 52 two-seat F-5Fs. They currently serve with at least eight squadrons of the Republic of China Air Force, formerly known as the Chinese Nationalist Air Force (Chung-kuo Kung Chuan), supplemented by more than 100 Lockheed F-104 Starfighters and at least 40 F-100 Super Sabres obtained from a number of different sources, mainly in Europe but including 27 TF-104Gs formerly used for Luftwaffe pilot training at Luke AFB, Arizona.

The star insignia is carried by all aircraft on the fuselage but only applied to the top surface of the F-5 wings. No tail flash is currently used, the only marking here being the aircraft serial number applied in white on the camouflage background colour. A four-digit code is prominently marked on the fuselage but this does not directly reflect the construction number — F-5E 400967 has 5110 on the fuselage, while 400968 has 5111 in a similar position; these were the tenth and eleventh aircraft, but 500334, the 55th example, carries 5161, as shown in the photograph at left.

modernity into this Far East air arm. By the national marking is the aircraft number and on the fin is the US serial. The Chinese characters mean 'in the centre'.

Tanzania

When Tanganyika and Zanzibar united in 1964 to form the United Republic of Tanzania, elements from both flags were combined to form the national emblem which is displayed on the fins of aircraft operated by the Tanzanian People's Defence Force Air Wing (Jeshi la Wananchi la Tanzania). The 'torch of freedom' roundel is located on the wings of most of the aircraft and on the fuselage it normally splits the JW prefix and the three-digit serial. The full serial of four numerals is usually applied on the fins of transport aircraft such as the DHC-5D Buffalo (JW9019 to JW9024) and HS.748 (JW9008 to JW9010). All the serials seen to date have been in the 9000 range, but confirmation as to the markings on Tanzania's few combat aircraft is still awaited. Types delivered include 24 Shenyang F-4 (MiG-17), 16 F-6 (MiG-19) and 16 F-7 (MiG-21), all from China.

Aircraft operated by the Tanzanian Police Air Wing and government machines carry civilian registrations prefixed 5H.

Thailand

After many years operating an almost bewildering mixture of types, many of them obsolete, the Royal Thai Air Force has embarked on a modernization programme which it hopes will forestall any attempt by troublesome countries to the east to invade it. Twelve F-16As have been ordered, with more required, and 47 RFB Fantrainers are being delivered to update the training fleet. The Northrop F-5Es already in service are painted in a disruptive 'aggressor' scheme of green, grey and light blue and carry miniature roundels on the rear fuselage, a small representation of the Thai flag on the fin and a five-digit serial number on the lower part of the fin. As with many Thai military aircraft, a separate number is carried by the F-5s as well as the serial; one example has 61670 on the fin and 10222 on the fuselage; the first three digits are thought to relate to the squadron number. The 1st Wing's F-5As have carried the unit's yellow and black leaping tiger on the forward fuselage; examples are F-5A 21257 and F-5B 38439.

The colours of the Thai flag are based on the Trairong ensign, introduced in 1917, in which red represents the nation, white the religion and blue the monarchy. On some aircraft, such as the C-130 Hercules, the roundel is applied in the US style, above the port wing and below the starboard, while on others (T-33s and SF.260s) it is above and below both wings. The fin flash is sometimes applied to the rudder rather than to the fin. Note that on Royal Thai Navy aircraft the tail flash comprises the official naval ensign, which incorporates a white elephant in its centre.

Numbering on Thai aircraft takes a variety of different forms. Sometimes the build number is used as the code for the machine such as the two Army-operated Shorts 330 aircraft 3098 and 3102 which are their production numbers. The application of different numbers from the serials has already been outlined above, while a third variation is the incorporation of the squadron number in the serial, an example being the Hercules of 601 Sqn — 60101, 60102 and 60103 — which were built as 4861, 4862 and 4863.

Thai language and numerals are often carried by support aircraft such as helicopters and transports, sometimes with the equivalent marking in English on the opposite side. Most maintenance markings are in English, signifying the large amount of US aid which has been given to Thailand over the past two decades.

0	1	2	3	4
0	๑	๒	๓	๔

5	6	7	8	9
๕	๖	๗	๘	๙

Togo

Originally German, more recently French, but independent since 1960, the Togo Republic uses the pan-African colours of red, yellow and green incorporating a white star signifying national purity. The flag is applied to the fin of aircraft flown by the Force Aérienne Togolaise and the roundel marking is carried on fuselage and wings. Six Brazilian EMB.326GB trainers and five ex-Luftwaffe Magisters received some years ago were supplemented more recently by five Alpha Jets, these constituting the country's sole combat capability. Three French Epsilon armed trainers have also been delivered recently. Aircraft are identified by civilian registrations applied on the rear fuselage. They are in the 5V-M series, the Alpha Jets being 5V-MBA to 5V-MBE and carrying the last two letters of the registration in large black capitals on the side of the forward fuselage.

Tunisia

Based on the Turkish flag (Tunisia was under Turkish rule in the mid-nineteenth century), the present national emblem forms the circular marking carried by all aircraft flown by the Republic of Tunisia Air Force. No fin marking is carried. Independent from France since 1956, Tunisia is a moderate Arab state and has only a small air arm which, until the arrival of some desperately needed Northrop F-5s, has soldiered on with much obsolete equipment. The 16 F-5Es and four two-seat F-5Fs have replaced some F-86 Sabres and have serials in the range Y92501, Y92502, etc. The aircraft are camouflaged and carry identification in the style of previous Tunisian aircraft such as the Macchi MB.326s which run from Y81. Two C-130 Hercules have also been delivered and these are marked with prominent civilian registrations in black on their fins, TS-MTA and TS-MTB (serials Z21011, Z21012).

Turkey

Part of NATO, Turkey is a recipient of large amounts of American aid to maintain the strength and effectiveness of the country's armed forces. Türk Hava Kuvvetleri is one of the main beneficiaries of this aid and its inventory includes F-104 Starfighters, F-100 Super Sabres, F-4 Phantoms and F-5s, due to be joined ▶

by F-16s. Many of the aircraft in combat use have been acquired from other air forces due to Turkey's poor financial situation, and without the agreement to licence-build the F-16, only the Phantoms and 40 late-version Starfighters bought from Italy can be considered as 'modern'.

Turkish military aircraft carry a fin flash duplicating the national flag and comprising a crescent moon and five-pointed star, traditional symbols of Islam. On the fuselage and wings, the original red Ottoman flag, outlined in white, was replaced in the early 1970s by the red and white roundel seen today. Individual aircraft identification is by its serial number if it is a former USAF or US Navy machine, or by the original construction number. A recent change has seen the use of a prefix digit which relates to the airfield where the aircraft is based. One example is an F-4E Phantom, whose serial 70295 is displayed in black at the base of the fin, with 1-295 in black outlined white on the intakes, the prefix indicating the base at Eskisehir (No 1 Air Base). Base numbers and names are: 1 Eskisehir; 2 Cigli; 3 Konya; 4 Murted; 5 Merzifon; 6 Bandirma; 7 Erhac; 8 Diyarbakir; 9 Balikesir; 10 Erkilet.

Sometimes, as in the case of the 20 ex-Luftwaffe Transalls of 221 Sqn at Erkilet, the base code number and the serial are split by the roundel; these aircraft also have the construc-

Above: Turkey became a member of the Phantom 'club' in 1974 and currently has more than 80 on strength. 01019 was the fourth F-4E delivered new from McDonnell Douglas and is shown before the application of unit codes and identification number to the engine intake. Camouflage is Vietnam style with night formation strips on nose, forward fuselage and fin.

tion number painted in black on a broad white band across the fin and rudder. Transport and support types such as the Bell UH-1H helicopters often carry the Air Force title in large letters on the fuselage. Badges had not featured on Turkish combat aircraft by May 1986, but they have been seen on the Transalls, the T-37s of the training unit at Cigli and on some Army-operated helicopters. What was probably an unofficial marking seen on the nose of a Dakota participating in the Turkish invasion of Cyprus in 1974 was a light blue outline of the island with three yellow parachutes superimposed. Turkish military aircraft wear various camouflage schemes, with many machines retaining the colours of their previous owner. Browns and tans are shades most favoured when aircraft are repainted, though there appears to be no set scheme for any particular type.

United Arab Emirates

In 1971 seven small states around the Persian Gulf combined to form the United Arab Emirates. They were Abu Dhabi, Dubai, Amman, Fujairah, Ras al-Kaimah, Sharjah and Umm al-Qaiwan: all contribute to the funding of the Air Force, and the new joint flag is carried by all military aircraft operated by the United Arab Emirates Air Force. Most UAEAF aircraft are based in Abu Dhabi, which is also the headquarters, and Dubai. The combat element operates Dassault-Breguet Mirage 5 fighter-bombers, the total of 32 received by 1977 including three for reconnaissance and two for training. The survivors of these will be supplemented and eventually replaced by 36 of the latest Mirage 2000s, delivery of which was expected to begin during 1986.

Meanwhile, the Mirages are painted in desert camouflage and carry serials in batches according to the version: Mirage 5AD and 5EAD fighter-bombers 401-412 and 501-514; reconnaissance Mirage 5RADs 601-603; and Mirage 5DAD trainers 201-203. These numbers are applied in black on the aircraft nose and repeated in Arabic characters, and when delivered the machines also carried A.D.A.F. alongside the roundel on the intake sides. Camouflaged in green and sand, the aircraft operate with the 1st Wing, UAEAF. BAe Hawk T.63s have been received to update the training force, the 16 aircraft bearing serials 1001-1016 and being assigned to the Abu Dhabi element of the UAEAF.

Dubai, further along the coast, has the same markings as Abu Dhabi; it has operated handful of MB.326s, both single- and two-seaters, for some years in the training and light attack roles. They carry large white serials 201-208 on the rear fuselage and will be supplemented by four MB.339s currently on order. Eight Hawk T.61s are in service marked 501-508. Carrying the full UAEAF insignia are the DHC-5D Buffalo transports which carry the title on one side of the fuselage roundel and the Arabic equivalent on the other. The six aircraft, 306-311, have the serials on the nose and rear fuselage and also under the wings.

Below: As part of the UAE armed forces, the Western Air Command (formerly Abu Dhabi Air Force) operates 16 Hawk T.63 advanced trainers at Al Dhafra. Colours are sand and light brown on the upper surface and light grey undersurfaces.

United Kingdom

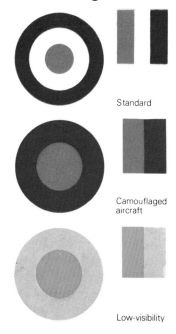

Standard

Camouflaged aircraft

Low-visibility

Markings and insignia of the British Services are many and varied and have prompted publication of a number of books devoted to the subject. This section deals only with the current markings applied to front-line aircraft operated by the Royal Air Force and the Royal Navy's Fleet Air Arm. Of all the insignia, the red, white and blue roundel has remained the symbol of British air power since its adoption by the Royal Flying Corps on December 11, 1914. It replaced the Union Flag on the fuselage sides and under the wings, and was a reversal of the French roundel. Six months later, in June 1915, red, white and blue rudder striping was introduced, setting the general pattern and positioning for British Service aircraft to the present day. Of course there have been variations in roundel size, application, style and location but the basic marking is still carried.

The application of markings and camouflage on UK military aircraft is specified and approved by the Ministry of Defence acting on behalf of the user service, and any change or modification has to be officially approved, or at least tentatively agreed down to squadron or unit level. Current orders state:

'Roundels are to be applied to the top and bottom surfaces of both main planes and on each side of the fuselage. A fin flash is to be applied to both sides of the fin. As an exception, roundel may be omitted from the undersurface of the mainplanes of tanker aircraft and the fin flash may be omitted from gliders constructed from plastic type materials.' In addition, 'aircraft serial numbers are to be applied on both sides of the fuselage'.

Roundel colours

The roundels on today's RAF front-line aircraft have had the white removed to form what is generally, but unofficially and incorrectly known as a B Type roundel, comprising red and blue with the former occupying half the diameter. Basic colours are matt or lustreless Post Office Red (BS381C-538) and Roundel Blue (-110), but to reduce marking visibility matt Pink and Pale Blue have been authorized to replace the original brighter shades. Roundel sizes vary according to aircraft type, but they are standardized at 54in (1,372mm), 48in (1,219mm), 36in (914mm), 18in

(457mm) and 12in (305mm) diameter overall. There are exceptions and changes will occur.

Fin flashes follow the same colour shades as the roundels and are usually located on the continuation of the fuselage top line, with the rear edge coinciding with the rear edge of the fin. The Jaguar provides a good example of this official requirement, while the Buccaneer and Phantom have their flash applied toward the top and near the leading edge respectively. Note that this type of marking is not displayed on Royal Navy or Army aircraft.

Serial numbers form the basis of aircraft identification in the British Services. The practice began in 1912, initially embracing aircraft of both the Royal Flying Corps and the Naval Wing and expanding subsequently to include the Army, and numbering has continued ever since. The present system consists of three digits in the 100 to 999 range, prefixed by two letters (AA to ZZ); a recent RAF example is ZE157, a Panavia Tornado F.3 fighter, but the range had reached ZF600 by mid-1986. All types of military aircraft are included, together with Service-operated hovercraft, and as a security measure there are gaps in the numbering to prevent accurate assessment of UK air strength. RAF aircraft are re-

quired to carry their serial number on each side of the rear fuselage or, in the case of the Tornado fighter, on the lower portion of the fin, forward of the flash. Standard serial height is 8in (203mm), usually in white on the current grey fighter scheme or black on the grey/green finish. Until the 1970s and the adoption of grey camouflage on RAF aircraft, almost all aircraft had their serials repeated on the lower surfaces of the wings. Some still do, particularly the larger types, but the accumulation of underwing weapons, fuel tanks and special purpose pods, all hung on pylons, obscured the serial to such an extent that it is beginning to disappear from combat aircraft such as the Phantom and Tornado fighter. On the other hand, Tornado strike aircraft retain the serial in black on the lower surfaces of the tailplanes. On the starboard side the tops of the letters and figures are nearest to the leading edge; on the port side, the tops are nearest to the trailing edge.

Phantom serials

An example of the serialling allocated to RAF combat aircraft is provided by the various blocks used for the McDonnell Douglas F-4 Phantom. This aircraft was ordered for both the RN (as the FG.1) and the RAF (FGR.2), but with the withdrawal of the last conventional carrier in 1979 all operational Phantoms were taken over by the latter Service. Phantom FG.1: XT595-598, XT857-876, XV565-592; Phantom FGR.2: XT852, XT853, XT891-914, XV393-442, XV460-501; Phantom F-4J (UK) ZE350-ZE364. Squadrons equipped with Phantoms are 19, 23, 29, 43, 56, 74, 92 and 111, plus 228 OCU; they are operational in the UK, West Germany and the Falkland Islands. ▶

Left: Tornados of 31 Sqn on a practice bombing mission from RAF Bruggen in Germany. On the noses and fins are the unit's emblems; at the base of the fins are the individual aircraft codes DE and DJ; under the tailplanes of the nearest machine can be discerned the serial number ZD844 and under the cockpit are the two sets of warning triangles.

British service aircraft designations provide an indication as to the role of the various types in use. The current list of functional prefixes is shown in the table, the abbreviation being followed by the Mark number, normally shortened to Mk, but more often than not replaced by a full point, as in Harrier GR.3:

UK aircraft designations

AEW	Airborne Early Warning
AH	Army Helicopter
AL	Army Liaison
AS	Anti-Submarine
B	Bomber
B(I)	Bomber (Interdictor)
B(K)	Bomber (Tanker)
B(PR)	Bomber (Photo Reconnaissance)
C	Transport
CC	Transport and Communications
D	Drone or unmanned aircraft
E	Electronic/Flight check
F	Fighter
FG	Fighter Ground Attack
FGA	Fighter Ground Attack
FGR	Fighter Ground Attack Reconnaissance
FR	Fighter Reconnaissance
FRS	Fighter Reconnaissance Strike
GA	Ground Attack
GR	Ground Attack Reconnaissance
HAR	Helicopter Air Rescue
HAS	Helicopter Anti-Submarine
HC	Helicopter Cargo
HT	Helicopter Training
HU	Helicopter Utility
K	Tanker
MR	Maritime Reconnaissance
PR	Photo Reconnaissance
R	Reconnaissance
S	Strike
T	Trainer
TT	Target Towing
TX	Training Glider
W	Weather

In addition to the aircraft serial, individual machines within a squadron carry a one- or two-letter code on the fin. This is either in a single colour (black, white, yellow or red) or in an outlined style (dark green outlined in yellow for 27 Sqn Tornados). Operational Conversion Units use a number of variations to distinguish their aircraft, including the three digits of the serial number, a sequential series of numbers usually beginning at 01, a code letter on each side of the fuselage roundel or, in the case of the Trinational Tornado Training Establishment, a letter and two digits.

Badges are a part of squadron tradition in many countries and the RAF is no exception. It maintains its past honours by retaining some kind of unit emblem on its aircraft despite the official requirement not to compromise the tone-down camouflage effect. Chequers, flashes, birds of prey and bars of colour help to brighten the dullness of the present-day finishes, but even before they are applied provision is made to ensure that they would disappear overnight should the need ever arise. Noses, engine intakes and fins are the usual location for this type of marking and some examples are illustrated. The present list of RAF front-line combat squadrons and their insignia is included here for completeness, but is only intended as an *aide mémoire* to enable a unit to be identified quickly and, it is hoped, accurately. There are many other squadrons in the RAF which have a combat role in wartime, such as the OCUs and Weapons Units, and it should be borne in mind that most markings are subject to change due to operational circumstances.

Maintenance and rescue

Other markings carried by front-line aircraft can be noted by walking round an example. Maintenance and rescue stencilling instructions are the most obvious, while less prominent are such essential items as wing-walk lines to prevent damage to moving parts and the small DTD paint specification numbers which usually occur at various points over the airframe. Some of the main NATO maintenance markings are illustrated in this section and can be found on aircraft operated by many of the world's military aircraft. The symbols are generally 4in (102mm) in their longest direction with the inscription in block capitals and numerals 1.5in (38mm) high except where otherwise specified. ▶

RAF operational, emergency and safety markings

Explosive actuated device

Variation for RAF Germany

Emergency canopy or hatch
release controls

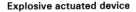

Fuselage break-in points

ASBESTOS GLOVES
STOWED HERE

FIRE
PANEL

Fire access panels

AXE STOWED HERE

FIRE EXTINGUISHER
STOWED HERE

Emergency equipment stowage

Powerplant inlet and/or exhaust

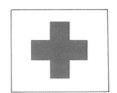

First aid kit stowage

Note that aircraft permanently based in West Germany have much stencilling duplicated in the German language; sometimes complete safety instructions are applied to RAFG Tornados, Phantoms and Harriers. Pilot's names are occasionally carried, mainly by the Unit Commanders, whose aircraft also have small rank pennants applied around the cockpit area (eg, two red horizontal stripes on light blue outlined in a dark blue arrow head for a Wing Commander).

Sea Harrier markings

Royal Navy Sea Harriers carry all the standard NATO markings, but there are some differences in national insignia compared with that applied to RAF aircraft. The most obvious is the lack of fin flashes, officially decreed not to be applied. In their place is the title ROYAL NAVY in 6in (152mm) high black letters along the base and under the squadron emblem, which is also in black outline form. At the fin tip is the carrier code letter, which in early 1986 conformed to the following: L — 800 Sqn, assigned to HMS *Illustrious*. Each aircraft of the unit carries a three-digit number on the intake (123-127). R — 801 Sqn, assigned to HMS *Ark Royal*. Intake codes are 000-004. VL — 899 Sqn, shore-based at Yeovilton for training. Intake codes 710-716 plus 721.

The badges comprise crossed swords within an 'arrow' marking

(800 Sqn), a trident (801 Sqn) and a winged fist (899 Sqn). Serials on Sea Harriers are difficult to find if you don't know where to look. They are actually located on the lower fin in black 3in (76mm) high letters and numbers in the XZ and ZA prefix ranges. Roundels have undergone a number of different styles since the Falklands war, but they appear to have standardised at 18in (457mm) in four positions — either side of the engine intakes and on the top surface of the wings. Note that like RAF aircraft Sea Harrier FRS.1s no longer carry underwing serials or roundels.

Right: An RAF Phantom crew prepares to start engines. The aircraft is from 111 Sqn, the unit emblem having been sprayed over a number of the smaller instructional markings. White lines act as guides for access to the cockpits, while the two small black circles are push buttons to actuate the canopy hydraulics.

Below: RAF Hawks in three different colour schemes. In light grey for the secondary intercept role is a T.1A from No 1 Tactical Weapons Unit at Brawdy with toned-down markings and the insignia of 234 'shadow' Sqn; aircraft 222 in green/grey is also from 1 TWU and wears 79 Sqn marks; and 239 is from 4 Flying Training School, Valley.

RAF front-line combat squadrons

Squadron	Aircraft	Identification marks
1 Sqn	Harrier GR.3/T.4	Winged 1 in white circle on nose
2 Sqn	Jaguar GR.1/T.2	Black 2 in white triangle on fin
3 Sqn	Harrier GR.3/T.4	Red & Green cockatrice on white circle and green/yellow bars
4 Sqn	Harrier GR.3/T.4	Red 4 with gold lightning flash on nose
5 Sqn	Lightning F.3/6/T.4	Green maple leaf on white circle
6 Sqn	Jaguar GR.1/T.2	Red can opener in circle; red zig-zag on fin
9 Sqn	Tornado GR.1	Dark green bat on fin
11 Sqn	Lightning F.3/6/T.5	Two dark brown & yellow birds on fin
12 Sqn	Buccaneer S.2	Fox's head on engine intakes
14 Sqn	Tornado GR.1	Winged emblem between blue & white bars
15 Sqn	Tornado GR.1	Roman XV in white on fin
16 Sqn	Tornado GR.1	Black & yellow bars and 'Saint' marking
17 Sqn	Tornado GR.1	Black & white arrow head on nose
19 Sqn	Phantom FGR.2	Blue & white checks on intake
20 Sqn	Tornado GR.1	Blue, red, white & green bars on nose
23 Sqn	Phantom FGR.2	Red eagle
27 Sqn	Tornado GR.1	Green arrow head; elephant badge on fin
29 Sqn	Phantom FGR.2	Red Xs on white background on nose and fin
31 Sqn	Tornado GR.1	Green & yellow arrow on nose; yellow star on fin
41 Sqn	Jaguar GR.1/T.2	Red cross of Lorraine on fin and intake
43 Sqn	Phantom FG.1	Black & white checks on fin
54 Sqn	Jaguar GR.1/T.2	Blue & yellow checks on intake
56 Sqn	Phantom FGR. 2	Red & white checks on fin
74 Sqn	Phantom F-4J (UK)	Tiger's head in circle on fin
92 Sqn	Phantom FGR.2	Yellow cobra on fin plus red & yellow checks
111 Sqn	Phantom FG.1	Black lightning flash outlined yellow
208 Sqn	Buccaneer S.2	Winged eye on fin
617 Sqn	Tornado GR.1	Red lightning flash on black fin band

United States of America

Standard

Low-visibility

Above: The US Air Force employs women for a variety of tasks ranging from ground trades to aircrew. This F-111D displays its basic data in standard form below the pilot's name stencil and also has the crew chief's rank and name.

Fifty states and the District of Columbia, which includes the capital city of Washington, are represented by the stars in the corner of the national flag of the United States, while the 13 stripes signify the original 13 colonies that rebelled against the British in 1775. Although the national flag is seldom carried in its entirety on US military front-line aircraft, the star and bar emblem forms the basic insignia for all US military types and was adopted in its current form in 1947. Construction of the national marking shape, using Insignia Red, Insignia White and Insignia Blue colours, is carefully formulated using the diameter of the circle, which is standardized in multiples of 5in (127mm); from this the sizes of the bars or rectangles and the five-pointed star are calculated.

Technical Orders for the application of this marking or variations of it state that it is to be located on 'each side of the aircraft fuselage, mid-way between the wing trailing edge and the leading edge of the stabilizer' and on the upper surface of the left wing and on the lower surface of the right wing'. These instructions are interpreted in various ways depending on the aircraft: the F-15 Eagle has the insignia on the fuselage, but adjacent to the variable angle intake, as does the F-111, while the shape of the F-16 dictates its application on the

rear fuselage and in inconspicuous outline form. In fact, the three colours associated with the marking are being used less and less as a result of the general toning-down process underway on today's US and NATO-assigned combat aircraft. Black outlines are increasingly used and almost no bright colours are now carried on the outside of American aircraft — at least as far as official markings are concerned.

To understand US military aircraft markings it is as well to outline how US designations are arrived at. Every aircraft introduced into service is given a number in the sequence of the type's role, a prefix letter indicating the role, a further letter after the model number to show the sub-type; the full designation also includes a block number and the initials of the manufacturer. For example F-111E can be deduced as the 111th fighter design and the fifth model (E) developed. The following type letters are currently in use (current examples are given in the table).

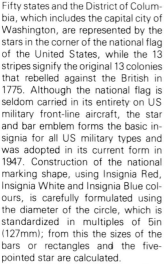

US type designations

A	Tactical support or attack (A-10)
B	Bomber (B-1)
C	Transport (C-130)
E	Electronic aircraft (E-3)
F	Fighter (F-111)
H	Helicopter (H-3)
O	Observation (O-2)
P	Patrol (P-3)
S	Anti-submarine (S-3)
T	Trainer (T-38)
U	Utility (U-17)
V	V/Stol (V-22)
X	Experimental (X-29)

Letters used as prefixes to the basic type indicators listed above such as DC-130 include the following:

US role prefixes

D	Drone director
E	Electronic equipment
H	Search and rescue
K	Tanker
L	Cold-weather operations
M	Permanently modified
N	Assigned special tests
Q	Drone
R	Reconnaissance
V	Staff transport
W	Weather reconnaissance
Y	Service test
Z	Project

The official aircraft designation can be found in an Aircraft Data Legend usually applied in black 1in (25mm) high letters on the left-hand side of the forward fuselage adjacent to the cockpit. This gives the type, model and series, the serial number, the aircraft production block number and the grade of fuel specified for the machine. Note that the manufacturer's or popular names for aircraft are specifically prohibited from use or display on any Air Force aircraft. Thus the name Eagle will not be found applied on the outside airframe of an F-15.

Aircraft serial numbers are allotted to USAF and US Army machines on a Fiscal Year (FY) basis, a system which has been in use since 1920. The FY runs from July 1 to June 30 and each serial has a two-digit prefix showing the year in which the aircraft, helicopter or even missile was ordered, followed by up to five digits which form the individual serial within that year's allocations. An example is General Dynamics FB-111A, serial number 67-7193 which was ordered in FY 1967 and was the 7193rd vehicle ordered in that year. The full serial appears small under the cockpit, but it is also applied on the fin in slightly abbreviated form as ▶

USAF tail markings

SJ code height is 24in (610mm) while the serial 1193 is 15in (381mm). This F-4E from the 4th TFW at Seymour Johnson also has the TAC badge on the fin.

77193 in light grey on a dark green background colour.

Tail presentation takes a number of forms. Within Tactical Air Command (TAC), United States Air Forces in Europe (USAFE) and Pacific Air Forces (PACAF), aircraft have the FY numbers in small digits beneath the letters AF, both in 6in (152mm) high characters, with the last three of the serial in 15in (381mm) high digits. Usually applied in black on camouflaged surfaces, the sizes change with the aircraft, some types having the large number in 6in or 8in (203mm) high digits. Sometimes four numbers of the serial are carried or the last digit of the FY and the first of the serial are presented small under the AF followed by the last three of the serial. The user designator USAF is applied on some aircraft fins, while larger types such as KC-135 tankers carry U.S. AIR FORCE along the nose in prominent characters; support and training aircraft also have this style of identity.

In addition to the serial, USAF combat aircraft carry two-letter tail codes. Introduced on tactical aircraft during the Vietnam war to aid identification of an aircraft's unit and base, the system has been retained and in general each code forms an abbreviation of the unit's base name, although this is not always the case. On most tactical aircraft, the letters are applied in 24in (610mm) high characters, usually in black but occasionally in grey or even white. For example the letters on the Cessna ▶

US Air Force tail codes

Code	Unit	Aircraft	Base
AD	3246 TW	A-10/F-4 F-15/F-16 F-111/RF-4	Eglin
AK	21 TFW/343 CW	A-10/F-15	Eielson/Elmendorf
AL	160 TFS	F-4D	Donnelly Field
AR	10 TRW	RF-4C	Alconbury (UK)
AZ	162 TFG	F-16	Tucson
BA	67 TRW	RF-4C	Bergstrom
BC	110 TASG	OA-37	Battle Creek
BD	917 TFG	A-10	Barksdale
BT	36 TFW	F-15	Bitburg (W. Germany)
CC	27 TFW	F-111	Cannon
CO	140 TFW	A-7	Buckley
CR	17 AF	F-15	Soesterberg (Netherlands)
CT	103 TFG	A-10	Bradley Field
DC	113 TFW	F-4	Andrews
DM	355 TTW	A-10	Davis-Monthan
DO	906 TFG	F-4	Wright-Patterson
ED	AFFTC	A-7/A-10 F-4/F-15 F-16/F-111	Edwards
EG	33 TFW	F-15	Eglin
EL	23 TFW	A-10	England
FF	1 TFW	F-15	Langley
FL	549 TASTS	OV-10	Patrick
FM	482 TFW	F-4	Homestead
FW	122 TFW	F-4	Fort Wayne
GA	35 TFW	F-4	George
HA	185 TFG	A-7	Sioux City
HF	181 TFG	F-4	Hulman Field
HI	419 TFW	F-16	Hill
HL	388 TFW	F-16	Hill
HO	49 TFW	F-15	Holloman
HR	50 TFW	F-16	Hahn (W. Germany)
IA	132 TFW	A-7	Des Moines
IL	182 TASG	OA-37	Peoria

IN	434 TFW	A-10	Grissom
KC	442 TFW	A-10	Richards-Gebaur
KE	186 TRG	RF-4C	Key Field
KY	123 TRW	RF-4C	Standiford Field
LA	405 TTW	F-15	Luke
LF	58 TFW	F-16	Luke
LN	48 TFW	F-111	Lakenheath (UK)
LV	4450 TG	A-7	Nellis
MA	104 TFG	A-10	Barnes
MB	354 TFW	A-10	Myrtle Beach
MC	56 TTW	F-16	MacDill
MD	175 TFG	A-10	Glenn Martin
MI	127 TFW	A-7	Selfridge
MJ	432 TFW	F-16	Misawa (Japan)
MO	366 TFW	F-111/EF-111	Mountain Home
MY	347 TFW	F-4	Moody
NA	474 TFW	F-16	Nellis
NF	602 TACW	OA-37	Davis-Monthan
NJ	108 TFW	F-4	McGuire
NO	442 TFW	A-10	New Orleans
NY	174 TFW	A-10	Hancock Field
OH	121 TFW	A-7	Rickenbacker
OK	138 TFG	A-7	Tulsa
OS	51 TFS	OA-37/F-4	Osan/Taegu (S. Korea)
OT	TAWC	A-10/RF-4C F-15/F-16	Eglin
PA	111 TASG	OA-37	Willow Grove
PN	3 TFW	F-4	Clark (Philippines)
PR	156 TFG	A-7	Muniz
PT	112 TFG	A-7	Greater Pittsburg
RG	AFLC	F-15	Robins
RS	86 TFW	F-16	Ramstein (W. Germany)
SA	149 TFG	F-16	Kelly
SC	169 TFG	F-16	McEntire
SD	114 TFG	A-7	Sioux Falls
SH	507 TFG	F-4	Tinker
SI	183 TFG	F-4	Springfield
SJ	4 TFW	F-4	Seymour-Johnson
SL	131 TFW	F-4	Lambert-St Louis
SP	52 TFW	F-4	Spangdahlem (W. Germany)
SU	25 TFS	A-10	Suwon (S. Korea)
SW	363 TFW	RF-4C/F-16	Shaw
TH	301 TFW	F-4	Carswell
TJ	401 TFW	F-16	Torrejon (Spain)
TX	924 TFG	F-4	Bergstrom
TY	325 TTW	F-15	Tyndall
UH	20 TFW	F-111/EF-111	Upper Heyford (UK)
VT	158 TFG	F-4	Burlington
VV	27 TASS	OV-10A	George
WA	57 FWW	A-10/F-4 F-15/F-16 F-111	Nellis/McClellan
WH	22 TASS	OV-10	Wheeler (Hawaii)
WI	128 TFW	A-10	Truax Field
WP	8 TFW	F-16	Kunsan (S. Korea)
WR	81 TFW	A-10	Woodbridge (UK)
WW	37 TFW	F-4	George
ZF	31 TTW	F-4/F-16	Homestead
ZR	26 TRW	RF-4C	Zweibrucken (W. Germany)
ZZ	18 TFW	RF-4C/F-15	Kadena (Okinawa)

USAF Command insignia

Strategic Air Command (SAC)

Tactical Air Command (TAC)

Space Command (SPACECOM)

Pacific Air Forces (PACAF)

US Air Forces in Europe (USAFE)

Alaskan Air Command (AAC)

Above: There are 13 major Commands in the US Air Force: shown here are the badges of the six responsible for front-line combat aircraft operation.

Below: The tail code identifies these F-15As as belonging to AAC's 21st TFW, based at Elmendorf; the consecutive serials indicate a special flight.

Representative F-15 squadron badges

1st TFW, 12th AF, Langley AFB, Virginia.

36th TFW, 17th AF, Bitburg, Germany

33rd TFW, 9th AF, Eglin AFB, Florida

OA-37 are 8in high due to the relatively small area available, while those on the C-130 Hercules were 36in (914mm). Orders state that the code will not overlap onto the rudder and where possible will avoid access panels, aerials and other markings on the fin. The current list of codes provides a guide to aircraft type, base and unit (pages 112-113).

Badges and unit insignia used by the USAF, and indeed the US Navy and Marine Corps as well, are a subject that is impossible to cover in any depth in a book of this size. Officially, USAF aircraft carry the badge of the user Command, be it SAC, TAC, PACAF, etc, usually located on the fin in 10in (254mm) or 18in (457mm) decals. In addition, the individual

Above: The 1st, 33rd and 36th TFWs were, respectively, the first operational F-15 unit, the first with MSIP F-15Cs and the first overseas F-15 wing.

squadron or wing badge is carried, often with further embellishments such as coloured stripes across the fin, squadron emblems, individual and certainly unofficial squadron markings of all shapes and sizes. Many flamboyant insignia are only for competitions such as Fangsmoke, Gunsmoke, Flag exercises or other 'friendly' tactical operations. Air National Guard units generally carry the official ANG emblem and the home State name of the Wing applied on a coloured stripe across the fin. Air Force Reserve units have recently been applying 'AFRES' in black on dark camouflage to conform with tone-down requirements. However, not all badges are in full colour. Like the AFRES markings, some insignia are in black outline only and plans are in hand for even the famous SAC badge to be applied in low contrast subdued colours that will blend with the present low-visibility camouflage. The badges of the six Major Commands that operate combat aircraft are illustrated opposite; others are:

Military Airlift Command Medium blue shield, dark-blue globe with yellow wings and arrows

Air National Guard Medium blue figure and two aircraft on white background, blue letters on white scroll

Air Force Reserve Dark blue shield with brown eagle and yellow wings. Red star and red centre. ▶

115

Other markings on USAF aircraft include pilot and crew chief names usually and officially applied on the left-hand side of the front fuselage below the cockpit in 2in (51mm) high black letters, but again this varies between units and even aircraft. Maintenance stencilling is in accord with NATO-agreed standards with basic instructional markings as shown in the UK section. Many TAC-operated aircraft have a patch on the front fuselage comprising a black or red lined area with the word ARMAMENT on which the various weapons are listed prior to a mission. Rescue and emergency markings continue to remain prominent although greys and black have sometimes replaced white and yellow to reduce visibility at distance.

Navy and Marine Corps

Markings on USN and USMC combat aircraft have succumbed to the official tone-down requirements to the extent that the red, white and blue of the national insignia have been replaced by a grey outline over the Compass Grey background colour, rendering it almost impossible to see at anything more than a few yards. Some aircraft still retain the older Light Gull grey upper surface scheme or variants of it and these have the older style of insignia. USN serials are generally known as Bureau Numbers (BuNos) and are allotted in sequence with up to six digits on current aircraft. They are not as prominent as those applied to USAF machines being located on the aft fuselage in small black or dark grey figures. Above the BuNo is the aircraft designation, such as A-7E/ 157585 on an LTV Corsair II.

More prominent are the tail codes carried by USN/USMC aircraft, but these differ from those on USAF types. Navy codes signify the Carrier Air Wing (CVW) to which the aircraft is attached, and by implication the squadron. Although there are variations, the average CVW is composed of two fighter squadrons (VF) with 24 F-14A Tomcats; two light attack squadrons (VA) with 24 A-7E Corsair IIs; one medium attack squadron (VA) with 10 or 11 A-6E Intruders; one tactical EW squadron (VAQ)

with four EA-6B Prowlers; one AEW squadron (VAW) with four E-2C Hawkeyes; one ASW squadron (VS) with ten S-3A Vikings; and one helicopter ASW squadron (HS) with six SH-3H Sea Kings. There are currently 13 Air Wings operational, one for each of the attack carriers; a 14th CVW is scheduled for activation in 1988 when the USS *Theodore Roosevelt* is commissioned.

Air Wing designations

The carriers and their Air Wings are divided into two Fleets, Atlantic and Pacific; the former have squadrons carrying codes prefixed A, while the Pacific units have N prefixes. The codes take many styles depending on the individual units, but the main ones and their carrier or shore base are listed below.

Carrier Air Wing tail codes

AA	USS *Saratoga*
AB	USS *America*
AC	USS *John F Kennedy*
AD	Shore-based at Oceana, Key West and Cecil Field
AE	USS *Independence*
AF	Shore-based at Dallas, Cecil Field, New Orleans and Atlanta
AG	USS *Dwight D Eisenhower*
AJ	USS *Nimitz*
AK	USS *Coral Sea*
BA	Blue Angels demonstration team (not applied to aircraft)
ND	Shore-based at Miramar, Alameda and Point Mugu
NE	USS *Kitty Hawk*
NF	USS *Midway*
NG	USS *Ranger*
NH	USS *Enterprise*
NJ	Shore-based at Miramar, Lemoore and Whidbey Island
NK	USS *Constellation*
NL	USS *Carl Vinson*
NM	Shore-based at Lemoore

Individual aircraft carry a three-digit number on the nose with the last two digits repeated on the fin; the number is also repeated on the flaps for ident during launching. These are in black or dark grey and are often outlined in white. The word NAVY or MARINES identifies the user Service, this being applied towards the rear of the airframe.

Squadron numbers are usually adjacent to the operator's name in the style 'VF-154'. The words JET INTAKE DANGER are applied in the appropriate position, previously in white and red but now in grey. The rescue and ejection seat triangle follow suit in the dullness of today's

markings. Squadron insignia are less colourful and on Navy aircraft are painted on the fin in greys.

US Marine Corps aircraft carry the legend MARINES to identify the user: on the new AV-8B Harrier II it is located on the base of the fin and on the top surface of the right-hand ▶

US Marine Corps tail codes

Code	Unit	Aircraft	Base
CF	VMA-211	A-4M	El Toro
CG	VMA-231	AV-8A	Cherry Point
CR	VMA-542	AV-8A	Cherry Point
DA	H&MS-32	OA-4M	Cherry Point
DB	VMFA-235	F-4S	Kaneohe Bay
DC	VMFA-122	F-4S	Beaufort
DN	VMFA-333	F-4S	Beaufort
DR	VMFA-312	F-4S	Beaufort
DT	VMA(AW)-242	A-6E	El Toro
DW	VMFA-251	F-4S	Beaufort
EA	VMA(AW)-332	A-6E	Cherry Point
EC	VMFA-531	F-18	El Toro
ED	VMA(AW)-533	A-6E	Cherry Point
ER	VMO-1	OV-10D	New River/Fulenma
HF	HMA-269	AH-1J/T	New River/Fulenma
KC	VMAT(AW)-202	A-6E	Cherry Point
KD	VMAT-203	AV-8A	Cherry Point
MA	VMFA-112	F-4S	Dallas
MB	VMA-142	A-4F	Cecil Field
ME	VMA-133	A-4F	Alameda
MF	VMA-134/VMFA-134	A-4F/F-4S	El Toro
MG	VMFA-321	F-4N	Andrews
MP	HMA-773	AH-1J	Atlanta
MU	VMO-4	OV-10A	Atlanta
QG	VMA-131	A-4E	Willow Grove
QP	VMA-124	A-4E	Memphis
QR	VMA-322	A-4M	South Weymouth
RF	VMFP-3	RF-4B	El Toro
SC	VMAT-102	A-4M/TA-4F	Yuma
SH	VMFAT-101	F-4J/S	Yuma
SM	HMA-369	AH-1J	Camp Pendleton
SN	HMA-169	AH-1T	Camp Pendleton
TQ	HMT-303	AH-1J	Camp Pendleton
UU	VMO-2	OV-10D	Camp Pendleton
VE	VMFA-115	F-4S	Beaufort
VK	VMA(AW)-121	A-6E	El Toro
VL	VMA-331	AV-8B	Cherry Point
VM	VMFA-451	F-4S	Beaufort
VW	VMFA-314	F-18	El Toro
WA	H&MS-12	OA-4M	Iwakuni
WD	VMFA-212	F-4S	Kaneohe Bay
WE	VMA-214	A-4M	Iwakuni
WF	VMA-513	AV-8A	Yuma
WK	VMA(AW)-224	A-6E	Yuma
WL	VMA-311	A-4M	El Toro
WP	VMA-223	A-4M	El Toro
WS	VMFA-323	F-18	El Toro
WT	VMFA-232	F-4S	Kaneohe Bay
YU	H&MS-13	OA-4M	El Toro

wing. National insignia are carried in outline form and all Marine types have the unit number with a prefix which incorporates the letter M such as VMAT-203 for the AV-8B training unit. Tail codes are carried, but are not abbreviations of the base name as in the USAF codes. The list of units only shows the combat elements; there are of course many support squadrons: the USMC alone has 38 with helicopters.

US Navy F/A-18 markings

AK indicates an Atlantic Fleet air wing operating from *Coral Sea*; the profile shows an F/A-18 of VFA-131 'Wildcats', the tail a Hornet of VFA-132 'Privateers'.

Representative F/A-18 squadron badges

VFA-113 'Stingers', USS *Constellation*

VMFA-314 'Black Knights', MCAS El Toro

VFA-131 'Wildcats', USS *Coral Sea*

Uruguay

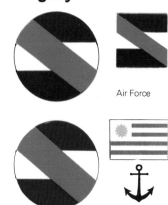

Air Force

Navy

This Spanish-speaking nation relies heavily on US aid for its military forces and this is manifest in particular in the Fuerza Aérea Uruguaya.

The main combat equipment comprises Cessna A-37B light attack jets and Lockheed AT-33s supplemented recently by six Argentinian Pucarás. The national circular marking is applied to the top surface of the port wing and the under surface of the starboard wing. In modified shape it is also carried on the rudder, sometimes extending the full length as on the Cessna 185s and C-47s, and as a small rectangle on the Cessna A-37s. These also have a badge applied to each side of the fin for Grupo de Caza No 2, the main fighter unit.

The FAU serialling system follows an accepted pattern: 001-099 for helicopters; 100-199 bombers; 200-299 fighters/advanced trainers; 300-399 trainers; 400-499 unused at present; 500-599 transports; 600-699 primary trainers; 700-799 communi-

cations types; 800-899 miscellaneous types. Numbers are applied both at the rear of the fuselage and at the nose on the A-37s and T-33s. Naval aircraft have the national flag on their tails, an anchor and national marking on the wings, with the legend AR-MADA on the rear fuselage.

Above: Top view of a Uruguayan AF A-37B light attack aircraft showing the camouflage pattern and the stencilling, the latter mainly consisting of 'no step' and 'no push' instructions in Spanish. Note the small rudder marking and the single roundel.

Venezuela

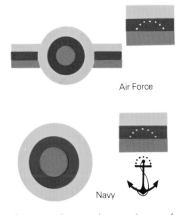

Air Force

Navy

Oil has been the saviour of Venezuela's economy and the high value of the commodity in the 1970s enabled the country's military forces to modernise, with the result that today Venezuela's air force (Fuerza Aérea Venezolana) is one of the most modern in Latin America. The FAV's fighter elements comprise two Escuadron or squadrons with GD F-16s, two with Mirage IIIs and 5s, and two with Canadair CF-5s, making a total of some 50 aircraft. Twenty BAC

Canberras form the strike component while 12 Rockwell OV-10 Broncos provide a light strike capability supported by some T-2E Buckeyes.

Markings on FAV combat aircraft take the form of the insignia seen above with types such as the Mirage and Bronco having the roundel applied in the US style standard positions — fuselage sides, port upper wing and starboard lower wing. The Canberras refurbished in the UK in the late 1970s were given a disruptive camouflage scheme over the top surfaces and had the fuselage roundel replaced by the standard fin insignia, comprising the yellow/blue/red stripes and the seven stars representing the number of provinces that formed the Venezuelan Federation in 1811.

The serialling of Venezuelan military aircraft appears to take a somewhat haphazard form. For instance, the Canberras carry four-digit numbers on their fins ranging from 0129, 1131 and 1183 to 6409, while individual Mirages are 1297, 7162 and 9510. Some aircraft carry the air force initials FAV on the star- ▶

Above: One of Venuzueala's two Mirage 5DV trainers displaying serial 5471 under the fin flash, two ejection seat triangles and the maker's name on the nose.

board top and port lower wing positions, and they are also applied to the rear boom of Bell helicopters operated by the Service. Transports have FUERZA AEREA VENE-ZOLANA on the fuselage. Maintenance and safety stencilling over the airframe is usually applied in Spanish such as RESCATE for Rescue.

The Venezuelan Navy can claim no front-line combat types, but does field some Grumman S-2 Trackers for anti-submarine use. These carry standard roundel and bar insignia on

wings and fuselage with the legend MARINA in large letters on the rear fuselage. Serials are prefixed AS for Anti-Submarinos and four-digit numbers run from 0101 in sequence but do not reflect the aircraft construction numbers. The serials follow a pattern, with Escuadron No 1 operating the Trackers, while Escuadron No 2 has transports numbered from 0201, Escuadron No 3 has helicopters from 0301, and so on. Aircraft in naval use also have a small anchor marking as well as the standard fin flash. Army-operated aircraft can be identified by an EV (Ejercito Venezolana) prefix to a four-digit serial, of which the first two indicate the year of purchase and the second two a sequential number.

Vietnam

Since the downfall of the South Vietnamese government in 1975 the unified Socialist Republic of Vietnam has endeavoured to spread its influence in surrounding countries: it now administers Kampuchea and is supporting Communist guerrillas in Laos and Thailand. The Vietnamese People's Air Force is part of the Army and has received an influx of modernized equipment in the form of MiG-23s and Sukhoi Su-22s, probably in exchange for the use of air and naval bases by the Soviet Forces. The yellow and red star and bar marking is usually applied on the fuselage and both surfaces of each wing, at least on the MiG-21s in service. Individual aircraft numbers consist of four digits applied on the nose, examples being 4326 and 5063 painted in red on the bare metal surface.

Yemen (North)

The Yemen Arab Republic Air Force operates Soviet-supplied aircraft including MiG-21s and Su-22s, although the country's brief flirtation with the West brought the supply of some Northrop F-5Es which are reportedly up for disposal. The roundel with the single green star is the main differentiating feature between the insignia of North and South Yemen: it is carried in the standard positions and the fin flash is a replica of the national flag. Aircraft serials comprise four digits, sometimes applied in Arabic characters.

Yemen (South)

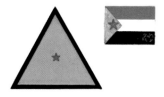

Previously known as Aden and independent since November 1967, the People's Democratic Republic of Yemen has been assisted in maintaining an air arm by the Soviet Union. Like its northern neighbour, South Yemen too has MiG-21s as well as some Su-22s and about 30 ageing MiG-17s. These all carry the triangular marking and the miniature flag insignia on the fin. Serviceability is thought to be relatively poor, and part of the force is believed to be in temporary storage.

Below: The likelihood of this Strikemaster still being operational is slim, but it does show South Yemen markings.

Yugoslavia

This socialist state has managed to maintain its independence despite having eastern borders with Warsaw Pact Hungary, Romania and Bulgaria. Equipment for the Jugoslav Air Force (Jugoslovensko Ratno Vazduhoplovstvo) has been procured from both East and West, the principal air defence type being the MiG-21, which has replaced the older F-86 Sabre originally acquired from US sources. Single-seat Jastreb fighter-bombers can be expected to be replaced by new Orao (Eagle) twin-engined attack aircraft as pro-

duction deliveries increase; both Jastreb and Orao wear green/brown disruptive camouflage while the MiGs are mostly in natural metal finish.

The present national insignia, incorporating a red socialist star, is a modification of the RAF roundel and is carried on wings and fuselage, while the flash is applied across the full width of the fin and rudder. Aircraft nose numbers are normally the last three digits of the serial number, which is carried in full on the fin. MiG-21s have been noted in the ranges 22500 and 25100, while Jastrebs are 24200 etc. Aircraft operated for the Jugoslav Government are civil registered, prefixed YU.

Below: Yugoslav AF MiG-21 with full-width fin flash and white exercise band around fuselage.

Zaire

Since 1971 the national flag of Zaire has featured the blazing torch emblem symbolizing the revolutionary spirit of the nation; it was first used by President Mobutu's Popular Movement of the Revolution established in 1967. Today, the marking is carried on the fin of the surviving Mirage 5M fighter-bombers which equip a single squadron in the Force

Aérienne Zaïroise. Although 14 were ordered originally it is believed that no more than nine or ten were actually delivered; of these about seven remain, serialled M401, M402, M403, etc, while three two-seat trainers received were allocated the marking M201, M202 and M203. No fuselage roundels are carried on the Mirages, but they have been seen on the MB.326 light attack aircraft and on other types such as the C-130H Hercules. The latter type also carries the air force title FORCE AERIENNE ZAÏROISE on the forward fuselage and civil registration letters towards the base of the fin (9T-TCA, 9T-TCB, etc). Serials on FAZ aircraft take the form of a role prefix followed by a

number such as FG-462 on an MB.326. As the construction number of this machine was 6462-203, it can be seen that serials are allocated on an internal basis.

Above: The first of three Mirage 5DM trainers in Zaire AF markings. The serial M201 is applied on the rear fuselage as well as on the nosewheel door.

Zambia

The Repubic of Zambia was officially formed in October 1964 and with British assistance established the Zambian Air Force. Initially a transport, liaison and training arm, the

ZAF moved into the Soviet sphere of influence toward the end of the 1970s, receiving 16 MiG-21s and some defensive ground-to-air missiles for the protection of the capital, Lusaka. Some Chinese Shenyang F-6s (MiG-19s) were also delivered and these two types constitute the country's combat element. The roundel and fin flash are applied in the standard positions, while the serials comprise three-digit numbers in blocks according to type prefixed by AF.

Zimbabwe

The serviceability and effectiveness of the Air Force of Zimbabwe has diminished to such an extent since the resignation and dismissal of almost all the white personnel that this once powerful counter-insurgency air arm is virtually non-operational. The three surviving

Canberras and the Reims-Cessna 337 Lynx light attack aircraft are currently stored, reliance for air defence being placed with the ten Hunters and seven Hawk trainers which are still believed to be flying.

The name Zimbabwe derives from a ruined city, believed to be of Bantu origin, and the national insignia features the Zimbabwe bird. This is applied to the fins of military aircraft such as the Hawk. Serials comprise four digits (2055, 2215 and 2250 are the stored Canberras), although recent deliveries such as the Hawks have three digits (600, 601, etc), in black on the rear fuselage.

Combat Camouflage

Camouflage is defined as 'disguise (of aircraft) effected by obscuring outline with splashes of various colours' and the colours applied to modern combat aircraft form an integral part of the machine's basic role. Although there are only seven colours in the spectrum, the camouflaging of aircraft involves all shades, with research and experimentation highlighting some as being more effective than others. As well as concealing and deceiving, colours also reflect the prevailing tensions arising from international relations around the world. Bright colours are often a sign of *détente,* while the application of drab camouflage on front-line aircraft may equally be an indication of a deterioration in one nation's relations with another country or countries.

In most cases modern camouflage is the result of extensive research by scientists using the very latest techniques in paint technology and application. Aircraft are painted and flown in the environment, be it over land or sea, at high or low level, for which the camouflage is designed. Results are analyzed, and orders are issued for the most effective scheme to be applied to the operational aircraft, either by the manufacturer when new-build aircraft are sprayed prior to delivery or at Service maintenance units when machines return for overhaul and a respray in the new colour or colours.

The visibility of an object, be it an aircraft or a tank, depends on its difference in colour and luminance or brightness from its background; luminance is the more important, as

Air superiority

Air defence is one area where a certain commonality exists when it comes to colours. In Western air forces, grey in various shades has been generally accepted as the most effective colour for fighter aircraft. Credit for much of the original research into the new air defence colours must go to the Defensive Weapons Department at the United Kingdom's Royal Aircraft Establishment, Farnborough. In conjunction with British Aerospace, the RAE conducted a series of experiments in the mid-1970s with a specially painted Hunter aircraft which proved that a machine painted overall matt light grey was more difficult to see against the sky than one with a multi-coloured disruptive scheme.

One problem noted by observers during the trials was that some areas of the airframe reflected more than others, while some were darker and throwing distinctive shadows. It was therefore decided to use more than one shade of grey on the aircraft, a lighter shade to brighten the darker areas and a darker shade to tone down the lighter areas, thus giving a uniformity of colour over the whole aircraft — a technique which became known as countershading.

The RAF Phantom force became the first to adopt this new scheme when the aircraft's role changed from offensive support to air defence. Tasked by the RAF's Central Tactics and Trials Organisation, the RAE formulated a subtle combination of Light Aircraft Grey (BS381C-627) for the undersurfaces with Medium Sea Grey (BS381C-637) on the top surfaces and Barley Grey (BS4800-18B21) on the outer wing panels. The result was

colours become less definite with increasing range due to the scattering of light by the atmosphere. The task of the camouflage specialist is to match as closely as possible an aircraft's colour and reflectance with those of its background, no easy task given that a fast-moving aircraft may have a terrain background one minute and a sky background immediately afterwards. Changing weather conditions can also alter the target and background quite considerably and quickly. Therefore, any

Above: Camouflaged Phantoms of 92 Sqn, RAF, formate with a lone grey example illustrating the effectiveness of the lighter colours for fighter operations.

camouflage applied to an aircraft must be a compromise and dependent mainly upon background priority. To illustrate the problems associated with colouring aircraft, this chapter is divided into the individual roles of current combat aircraft.

RAF Tornado F.3

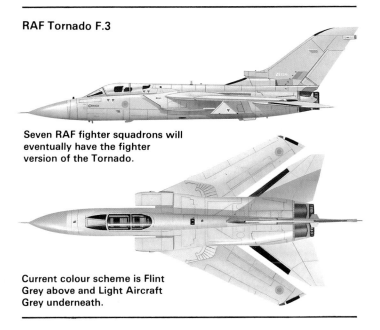

Seven RAF fighter squadrons will eventually have the fighter version of the Tornado.

Current colour scheme is Flint Grey above and Light Aircraft Grey underneath.

dramatic: during mock combat aircrew experienced extreme difficulty in finding the aircraft, particularly at high level.

In 1979 the RAF officially adopted the new scheme for the Phantom and later, in slightly modified form, it was applied to the Lightning and Tornado interceptors. In order not to compromise the whole effect, the mass of external stencilling on the aircraft was reduced (on the Phantom this involved eliminating some 600 servicing instructions of 700 originally carried), white remained absent from the insignia and pastel shades were substituted for the previously bright red and blue colours. A reduction in the size of the main markings was also introduced.

However, despite tactical requirements, RAF fighters continue to operate with squadron badges and markings prominently displayed on tails and fuselages. Applied in bright colours, these form an important part of the Service's *esprit de corps*, but they do little to aid the painstaking efforts of the camouflage specialists. At times of crisis they would be removed, along with all the other markings which an enemy might use to gain a visual advantage in close air combat.

More recently, RAF Hawk T.1As assigned to the point defence role have begun adopting a scheme of Medium Sea Grey over the top surfaces and Barley Grey underneath; again; markings are small and few in number. During the trials which led to the adoption of this scheme, a black dummy canopy was painted on the underside of the forward fuselage to add to confusion in combat. The effectiveness of this device was such that in mock combat flying became extremely hazardous, as pilots were unable to tell which way up the Hawk with the false canopy was. With safety compromised the marking was painted out, but it remains an effective tactical option should the need ever arise.

US approach

The American approach to modern fighter camouflage has followed similar lines. With a new range of advanced combat aircraft under development, both the US Air Force and the US Navy undertook trials in the early 1970s to determine the best colours for the fighter role. Air Superiority Blue was one colour that was much favoured by the USAF in early research, and prototype F-15s and F-16s appeared in this attractive colour. However, it was not adopted: instead, American research came to the same conclusion as the RAE. Grey was the common factor and the McDonnell Douglas and General Dynamics paint shops at St Louis and Fort Worth respectively received instructions to apply shades of grey in carefully formulated schemes to new production F-15s and F-16s.

On the F-15, a countershaded system of two greys (Compass Ghost Greys FS595a 36375 and 36320) covers the aircraft in the form

Below: USAF F-16s of the South Korea-based 8th TFW pictured during Exercise Team Spirit '85. Colours are Dark Grey (saddle area), Middle Grey (nose and fin) and Underbelly Grey (undersides).

USAF F-15C Eagle

Bitburg, West Germany, is the base for this F-15 Eagle, which carries the standard USAF scheme for this air superiority fighter.

Officially called high and low reflectance grey, the scheme consists of Dark Compass Ghost Grey (FS 36320) and Light Compass Ghost Grey (FS 36375).

Luftwaffe F-4F Phantom

Tactical camouflage on a Luftwaffe F-4F Phantom of JG 74.

The Germans derived the sharp-
angled 'splinter' scheme from
their aircraft of World War II.

shown in the accompanying illustration. Demarcation lines are relatively
easy to see at close range, but in the
air the two colours merge to conceal
the machine against the background. In June 1978 the USAF
selected a three-tone grey scheme
for the F-16, comprising Dark Grey
on the saddle area, Middle Grey on
the nose and fin, and Underbelly
Grey on the undersurfaces (FS

36081, 36118 and 36375 respectively), while the semi-gloss black
radome on early aircraft gave way to
Middle Grey when mock combat
confirmed that such a heavily con-
trasting area totally compromised
the whole effect.

This three-tone scheme became
the standard General Dynamics
layout for all F-16s unless customers
specified otherwise and some did —

Above: In line with other air forces, the Luftwaffe is now repainting its F-4Fs in lighter shades of grey, this example being operated by JG 71.

Below: A US Navy F-14A Tomcat about to launch from the USS *Saratoga*. 'Grey on grey' best describes the scheme, the red fin flash providing the only colour.

Norway, for example, requested a single all-over colour, namely Middle Grey, for her aircraft, as they would have to operate over both land and sea and at high and low altitude.

US naval schemes

The US Navy and Marine Corps tested a number of different schemes before the adoption of three shades of grey in a subtle combination. At one stage, artist Keith Ferris evolved a hard-edged zig-zag pattern of greys for use on the F-14 Tomcat (he produced another for the USAF F-15), but this was aimed at deception rather than concealment and the proposal was not accepted. Codes, national markings and squadron insignia are all applied in subdued form over the latest standard USN scheme, and for the present the famous flamboyant colours associated with the American Navy have had to give way to more practical considerations (see also the section on Naval colours).

Fighters in other countries are also sporting new, lighter camouflage. Dutch F-5s are receiving a counter-shaded scheme similar to the F-16s,

Swedish Viggen fighters have a light grey in total contrast to the green splinter scheme previously applied, and Federal German F-4F Phantoms are steadily receiving a new combination of no fewer than six colours (RAL7030 Steingrau, 7039 Quartzgrau, 7009 Grüngrau, 7012 Basaltgrau, 7037 Staubgrau and 7035 Lichtgrau).

The French Air Force shunned the application of paint to its interceptors for years, preferring to retain a natural metal finish. However, the arrival of the Mirage F.1 and the new Mirage 2000 highlighted the need for some kind of concealment at altitude — after all, metal gives numerous reflections when unpainted. The result was a blue-grey colour over the upper surfaces, but retaining the natural metal underneath. Mirage 2000s are being delivered to the squadrons in two greys, and a recent modification to the scheme is the overpainting of the black nose radome with light grey to improve overall concealment at high altitude.

The Soviet, East European and Chinese air arms are more conservative than their Western counterparts when it comes to colour schemes. With few exceptions their fighter aircraft have shown no individualism in terms of squadron markings, and camouflage is generally only applied to close support types. Their fighters are mostly Soviet in origin and so huge are the production requirements of Russian manufacturing plants that aircraft are often delivered in natural metal finishes or given a light grey colour for protection rather than airborne concealment.

Paint finishes

As gloss surfaces exhibit glint, which is probably the greatest clue to detection, the ideal paint finish on fighter aircraft, or any combat aircraft for that matter, is matt or, in US parlance, lustreless. However, a major problem with this type of finish is the ease with which it can be contaminated. Aircraft have to be serviced and ground crew need to gain access to parts of the airframe on a regular basis, the result being scuff marks and a quick deterioration of

Above: Sweden experimented with various shades of grey and ended up with the colour seen here. The aircraft is a JaktViggen or fighter JA37 Viggen of the crack F13 Wing based at Norrkoping. On the fin is the unit badge and the engine intake has the FARA or Danger sign prominently displayed. The raked fin tip identifies the JA37 variant.

the surface. Add the occasional spillage of oil and lubricants, and you have an aircraft with the appearance of a 'scrap yard queen' no self-respecting squadron would want to be associated with.

One answer in recent years has been to resort to a semi-gloss finish, which preseves the appearance of the machine but does little for the camouflage requirement; another has been the formulation of a cleaning material which removes all external marks and preserves the vital finish. However, a unit commander should be in no doubt that a scruffy aircraft returning from a mission is better than a smart one that doesn't.

Soviet MiG-31 'Foxhound'

'Blue 21' became the first MiG-31 'Foxhound' to be widely seen by the West after it was photographed off northern Norway in 1985.

The aircraft shows no concession to individual markings apart from the large Bort number and the prominent national insignia.

Ground-attack

The requirements for concealment at low-level are similar to those for air defence: aircraft need colours that match the terrain they fly over or a scheme that will reduce the chances of their being seen by an enemy. Based on disruptive patterns used during the Second World War, RAF front line aircraft were given a scheme of Dark Green/Dark Sea Grey on the upper surfaces and Light Aircraft Grey or Silver undersides from 1953 until he early 1980s. These colours were intended to hide the aircraft on the ground when dispersed around an airfield as well as when flying on operations. The only change to this scheme in recent years has been the elimination of the Light Aircraft Grey and its replacement by the top surface colours wrapped around in pattern form under wings, fuselage and tail. Harriers, Jaguars and Tornados have all been given this form of colouring.

While that old standby grey has proved to be the most adaptable colour for aircraft camouflage, certainly against the sky and, some experts would argue, also against a multi-coloured landscape such as the terrain in central Europe, the RAF has decided to adopt a new finish for its Harrier force. This comprises NATO Dark Green in a semi-matt or satin finish over the top surfaces and Litchen Green (BS4800-12B25) on the undersurfaces. Current plans call for all GR3s and the latest GR5s to be sprayed in these colours, but the remaining reconnaissance/attack Jaguars and Tornado strike aircraft (see under Penetration section) will retain their present two-colour coverage.

Below: RAF Harriers are being given a new scheme of Litchen Green and NATO Dark Green as shown on 'AF' of 4 Sqn.

RAF Harrier GR.3

Harrier GR.3 of 233 OCU, based at RAF Wittering, in standard Dark Green/Dark Sea Grey.

The red markings in the centre of the fuselage indicate a No Step area for ground crews.

USAF attack aircraft changed from their natural metal finish of the 1950s and early 1960s to the Southeast Asia camouflage of two greens and tan with America's increasing involvement in the Vietnam war. The withdrawal from SE Asia and the US commitment to Europe meant the reassignment of aircraft to bases in West Germany and the UK with the result that it was decided to evolve paint schemes more in keeping with the central European theatre.

European One

One type with a vested interest in low-level survival is the Fairchild A-10 Thunderbolt close-support aircraft. Capable of carrying up to 7 tons of external ordnance and designed to fly round trees instead of over them, the A-10 was used in trials to determine an optimum colour scheme for European-based units. After much experimentation, the result was a disruptive pattern applied over the whole aircraft of Dark Olive Green, Dark Green and Dark Grey (FS 34103, 34092 and 36081 respectively) which was unofficially dubbed 'lizard' but is properly the European One scheme. There appear to be variations to this very dark scheme with FS 36118 replacing 36081 on some aircraft and the grey

USAF A-10 Thunderbolt

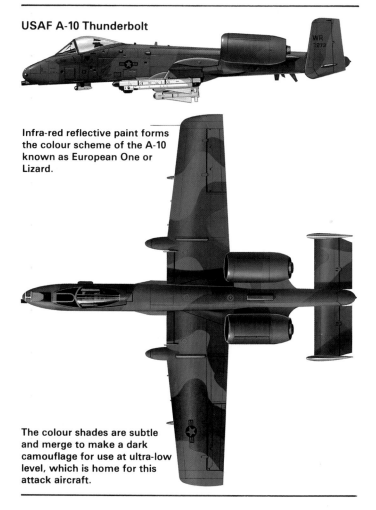

Infra-red reflective paint forms the colour scheme of the A-10 known as European One or Lizard.

The colour shades are subtle and merge to make a dark camouflage for use at ultra-low level, which is home for this attack aircraft.

changing in shade to present what often looks like a different camouflage altogether. Transports like the Lockheed C-5A/B Galaxy and C-141 Starlifter have also received the modified European One scheme, a costly and time-consuming operation, and it is no surprise to learn that the USAF is now considering a change for these aircraft to a more practical and less complicated scheme. It should also be noted that although there is an official three-colour pattern for each aircraft, changes occur from one machine to another.

Below: The SE Asia camouflage pattern wraps round the whole aircraft, as shown on this two-seat A-7K of the 162nd TFG, US ANG, based at Tucson, Arizona.

Luftwaffe Tornado

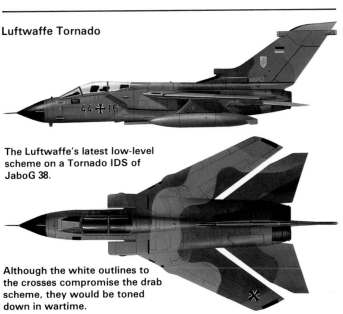

The Luftwaffe's latest low-level scheme on a Tornado IDS of JaboG 38.

Although the white outlines to the crosses compromise the drab scheme, they would be toned down in wartime.

Luftwaffe Alpha Jet

Alpha Jet of JaboG 43 in the scheme carried until 1985, when a change was ordered to incorporate more green over all surfaces.

The only marking that is 'unofficial' on this aircraft is the yellow and black stripes at the fin tip indicating participation in a NATO Tiger Meet.

West Germany's main attack aircraft is the Panavia Tornado, which is replacing the F-104G Starfighter, and early aircraft from the Panavia production line were given a disruptive colour scheme of Black, Yellow-olive (RAL6014) and Basalt Grey (RAL7012) over the top surfaces plus Silver Grey (RAL7001) on the lower surfaces. While this was generally in keeping with the usual dark colours employed by most air arms, the Luftwaffe decided that a finish incorporating more green was required. The result was a scheme not unlike the American European One combination and formed of an overall 'wrap-round' camouflage of Dark Grey, Dark Green and Medium Green, with the black radome being retained. Luftwaffe Tornados are operated in the counter-air, anti-armour and strike roles, as are the examples flown by the Italian Air Force. The latter have a disruptive pattern of NATO Dark Green (BS381C-641) and NATO Dark Grey (638) over the top surface and Silver on all lower surfaces.

Conflicting requirements

From the foregoing, it is plain that there is no conformity when it comes to aircraft colour schemes. Even NATO with all its STANAGs (Standard Agreements) has not managed to formulate a basic camouflage pattern or even a directive to member nations that their aircraft should adopt certain colours, and while there certainly are NATO colours, they are not used by all the alliance's air arms. Conspiring against the much sought after standardization are the often very different requirements each nation has for its aircraft. Some have a purely overland role, but the dense forests of northern Europe are quite different from the mountainous terrain in Greece and Turkey. For the dual-role mission involving intercept and ground-attack, a compromise colour scheme will be sought, while over-water flying demands an altogether

Soviet Mi-24 'Hind-D'

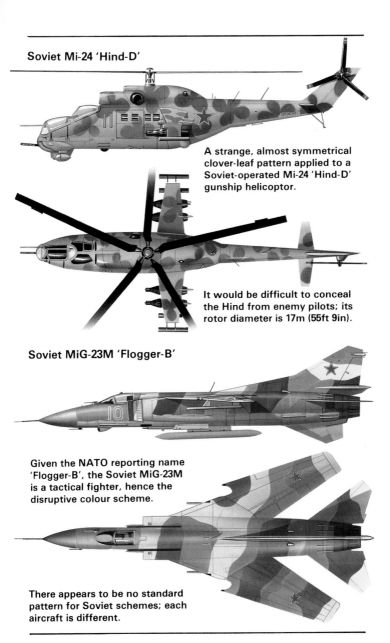

A strange, almost symmetrical clover-leaf pattern applied to a Soviet-operated Mi-24 'Hind-D' gunship helicoptor.

It would be difficult to conceal the Hind from enemy pilots; its rotor diameter is 17m (55ft 9in).

Soviet MiG-23M 'Flogger-B'

Given the NATO reporting name 'Flogger-B', the Soviet MiG-23M is a tactical fighter, hence the disruptive colour scheme.

There appears to be no standard pattern for Soviet schemes; each aircraft is different.

different approach to the problem.

Over the border in the East, the numerous ground-attack regiments which form a large proportion of the Warsaw Pact air forces have standardized on aircraft types if not on colour schemes. MiG-21s, -23s and -27s, along with Sukhoi Su-17s and a few new Su-25s, constitute the vast majority of the attack force, and almost all employ multi-coloured camouflage schemes made up of dark greens, browns, greys and tans.

Precisely how these colours were arrived at will probably never be known for sure. They have a similarity with the American Southeast Asia schemes, but whereas there was some uniformity in those, the Soviet Union and Warsaw Pact seem to have no basic pattern, though matching between aircraft does sometimes occur. The undersurface colour is usually centred on light blue or light grey, the demarcation line being either wavy or straight.

Soviet combat aircraft destined for export to overseas air forces are sprayed in camouflage before despatch. Libyan and Indian MiG-23s have very similar colours, as do the Mil Mi-24/25 attack helicopters flown by the Afghan and Algerian air arms; those supplied to Nicaragua, however, have a predominantly green disruptive scheme for operations over the jungle.

Desert colours
Middle East air forces have traditionally employed a desert finish which during World War II was generally called 'sand and stone' when applied to Allied Spitfires, P-40s, Hurricanes and other types. The Luftwaffe sprayed its Bf 109s and Bf 110s brown over the top surfaces with light blue underneath. Variations on this ranged from large splotches of dark brown or green over the base colour to mottled green

as the North African war drew to a close in the more verdant terrain of Tunisia.

Nowadays, countries like Israel retain desert camouflage for their attack aircraft while grey schemes are used by the interceptors. Kfirs, A-4 Skyhawks and F-4 Phantoms of the Heyl Ha'Avir carry patterns made up of sand, tan and medium green with

Sultan of Oman's Air Force Jaguar

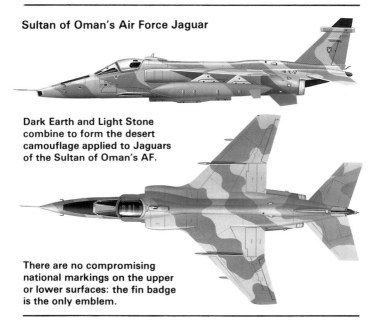

Dark Earth and Light Stone combine to form the desert camouflage applied to Jaguars of the Sultan of Oman's AF.

There are no compromising national markings on the upper or lower surfaces: the fin badge is the only emblem.

pale blue undersurfaces, a combination jokingly referred to as 'Cafe au lait'. Often compromised by large black and orange ID triangles (on the Kfirs), the camouflage proves effective for low-level concealment as well as breaking up the aircraft outline on the ground at airfield dispersals. Further west, Egyptian aircraft are painted in a number of different

Above: Japan received 14 RF-4EJ reconnaissance Phantoms. This example carries one of the early three-tone colour schemes.

finishes, from an overall sand colour to quite dark schemes on the large fleet of MiG-21s; green, tan and brown are, again, common top surface colours.

Heyl Ha'Avir Kfir-C7

Israeli Kfirs assigned the intercept role carry a grey scheme as seen here on aircraft 824.

The aircraft's Mirage III ancestry can be recognized from the plan view, although the foreplanes are innovative additions.

In the Far East, there are few startlingly different colours to relieve the predictability on the camouflage scene. Australian-operated Mirages have a semi-matt two-tone finish of Extra Dark Sea Grey (BS381C-640) and Olive Drab (BS381C-298) over the top surfaces with Light Gull Grey (FS 26440) underneath; leading edges of wings, fin and engine intakes are glossy to prevent erosion, common practice with the matt finishes. Recently, some Mirages have been appearing in a new blue-grey finish not unlike some of the NATO schemes now in use. RAAF F-111s have the US Southeast Asia finish of two greens (FS 34079 and 34102) and tan (30219) with black (37038) undersides. Replacing the Mirages are 73 licence-built F-18 Hornets, but these new aircraft will have none of the drab disruptive patterning of the older aircraft, the RAAF preferring to retain the grey finish currently being applied by McDonnell Douglas to US Navy aircraft. Interestingly enough, each Hornet is given a total of 70 litres of paint — 38 litres sprayed on the undersurfaces and 32 on the top. The matt grey is applied in two coats, with two extra coats on the leading

Above: Engine runs on the seventh A-4 Skyhawk for Malaysia prior to delivery. As the aircraft is used for the low-level attack role, a disruptive scheme has been applied, as seen in this view of M32-07.

edges, and together with the application of markings and insignia the painting takes some ten days per aircraft.

Chinese colours

The Chinese Air Force, one of the world's largest, has used dark green as the standard finish for tactical aircraft for many years, although this practice now seems confined to helicopters and trainers. As outlined in the previous section, Chinese combat types are often unpainted, though in recent times ground-attack machines have been noted in a diagonally-striped scheme of green and brown with light blue underneath. This was first seen on A-5 Fantans during the brief war with Vietnam in 1979 and was presumably evolved for operations over the border area between the two countries, but similar schemes have been seen since.

Penetration

Long-range, low-level penetration of an enemy's defences is the task of a select few specialized types. Equipped with the latest electronics to defeat and confuse high-powered early-warning radars and carrying the most lethal and destructive weaponry, these machines constitute one of the biggest threats faced by defensive forces, but such is the very high cost of developing and operating this type of aircraft that they are on the inventories of only a few nations.

Taking over the UK strategic bomber role from the withdrawn Vulcans is the RAF's fleet of new Tornado GR.1s. Based on airfields in the UK and West Germany these carry both active and passive ECM but also rely on disruptive camouflage for visual concealment. Colours are matt Dark Green (BS381C-641) and Dark Sea Grey (638) over the whole aircraft apart from the radome, which is black. Eleven RAF squadrons will eventually operate Tornados, among them a dedicated reconnaissance unit.

Also based in Europe are two USAF Tactical Fighter Wings equipped with F-111E and F versions of the early F-111As which saw service in Vietnam. The matt black undersurface colour first applied in Southeast Asia for night attacks has been re-tained, as has the uppersurface camouflage of two greens and a tan which formed the SE Asia scheme. To date there have been no moves to adopt the European One colours for these aircraft or for the F-111s and FB-111s stationed in the USA.

In fact, the only variant of this low-level aircraft which exhibits a change of colour is the EF-111A Raven electronic warfare machine, identified by the prominent fin tip pod and the long canoe-shaped radome under the fuselage. These aircraft have a two-grey scheme compatible with their medium- to high-altitude operation, although they are also designed to accompany deep penetration strike aircraft to high-priority targets well inside enemy territory.

The Soviet equivalent of the F-111 is the Sukhoi Su-24. Like its American counterpart it has two crewmen, two engines and swing wings, but it is smaller, lighter and somewhat less capable. However, many hundreds of these low-level attack bombers form the Soviet Air Force's tactical 'punch', being based along the Eastern Bloc border and in the Far East. The only photographs

Below: An air defence Hawk of the RAF formates with a Tornado of 617 Sqn displaying its current low-level camouflage colours.

of Su-24s so far released show aircraft painted in a medium grey over the upper surfaces with a light grey underneath. Nose radomes appear to be light grey, as does the leading edge of the fin. Whether this finish incorporates any kind of radar reflectivity or even anti-infra-red properties must remain purely speculative for the present.

At the strategic level, only the United States and the Soviet Union have aircraft which can be termed truly long-range strategic bombers. The USAF is currently receiving the Rockwell B-1B, 100 of which will be in service by 1989, and the chequered career of this design can be traced via the three main colour schemes carried by different examples since the first prototype was completed in 1974.

B-1 colours

The first three B-1A prototypes were given an anti-flash white finish to

USAF B-1B

The dark radar reflective colours on the B-1B give the aircraft a particularly sinister appearance. Markings are few and those that are present are mostly small and unobtrusive.

Breaking the sombre scheme are the air refuelling guide markings on the nose, the wing-walk lines and the single national emblem.

cope with the high-altitude supersonic role as well as the low-level near-sonic mission. Production was cancelled in 1977 although development work continued on various systems until the programme was resurrected by President Reagan as the B-1B; meanwhile, a sand and green finish was applied to the fourth prototype B-1A and it was generally believed that SAC would adopt this for the production examples. However, when the first B-1B rolled out in 1984, it was sprayed in the European One scheme and this appears to be the standard finish for the type.

Much lighter shades of green, brown and tan are applied to SAC B-52G and H Stratofortress bombers to help conceal these large machines in flight, though given their size it would seem unlikely that camouflage alone will hide them from enemy eyes, hence the extensive use of ECM and active countermeasures in the form of chaff and decoys.

The Soviet Air Force has done little to camouflage its long-range bomber force and electronics aircraft. Most of the Tu-95 and Tu-142 Bears intercepted around NATO countries are finished in the natural metal they were built in except for some Naval-operated examples which have a two-tone grey finish divided by a straight line along the sides of the

Left: Concealing an aircraft the size of the B-52 can be difficult, although the scheme on this G version can be effective over some types of terrain.

Below: The Raven is the only version of the F-111 family to have grey colours. This is the first example assigned to Europe.

fuselage. Tupolev Tu-22M 'Backfires' and Tu-16 'Badgers' often appear in grey colours, but these are again believed to be Naval machines rather than Air Force.

France's *Force de Frappe* strategic bomber fleet of Mirage IVs has been given disruptive camouflage for the low-level nuclear attack role. Green and grey are the colours used and smaller roundels have been applied to the fuselage and wings.

Soviet Su-24 'Fencer-C'

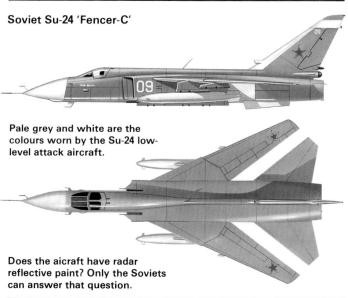

Pale grey and white are the colours worn by the Su-24 low-level attack aircraft.

Does the aicraft have radar reflective paint? Only the Soviets can answer that question.

Soviet Tu-22M 'Backfire'

Soviet Naval Air Force aircraft often have a two-colour camouflage in a layout exemplified by this Tu-22M 'Backfire'.

At low level against the sea the blue-grey upper surface colour would be quite effective in concealing the aircraft's shape from enemy eyes.

Naval colours

Over-water operations have traditionally dictated certain colours for naval aircraft. These range mainly between light grey and dark blue, though a brief look back at history will show that green has been used in the past, particularly during World War II. Luftwaffe Ju 88s flying in the anti-shipping role carried a 'wave mirror' scheme of light blue snaking lines applied over the basic two-green splinter camouflage, although it is difficult to determine how effective this was in concealing the aircraft from those they were attacking.

South Atlantic experience

For the Royal Navy's Fleet Air Arm, the 1982 South Atlantic War was a milestone in a number of ways, including the noticeable change in the camouflage and markings carried by its aircraft. The withdrawal of the FAA's fixed-wing aircraft element (Phantoms, Buccaneers, Sea Vixens and Gannets) was occasioned by the retirement of the Navy's last conventional carrier, HMS *Ark Royal*, in 1979. However, the fixed-wing aspect did not disappear as in the

same year the FAA accepted the first of its STOVL Sea Harriers. These were finished in the long-established scheme of semi-gloss Dark Sea Grey (BS381C-638) over all upper surfaces and gloss white underneath, while roundels were the conventional red, white and blue and prominent unit insignia decorated the fin.

Then, in 1982, came the brief but hard-fought war with Argentina over the Falkland Islands. The Sea Harrier was the only tactical fighter available to the British Task Force, and 20 aircraft, resplendent in the colours outlined above, sailed aboard the ski-jump-equipped carriers *Hermes* and *Invincible* on April 5, 1982. During their transit south the aircraft were toned down, with the white undersurfaces being given a coat of gloss Extra Dark Sea Grey, the white in the roundels overpainted in blue, and crew names and unit insignia being painted out altogether. Later aircraft ferried out from the UK were finished in semi-matt Medium Sea Grey (BS381C-637) over the top surfaces and fuselage, with semi-matt Barley Grey (BS4800-18B21) on the wing

Royal Navy Fleet Air Arm Sea Harrier FRS.1

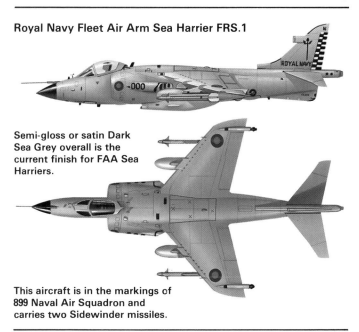

Semi-gloss or satin Dark Sea Grey overall is the current finish for FAA Sea Harriers.

This aircraft is in the markings of 899 Naval Air Squadron and carries two Sidewinder missiles.

and tailplane undersurfaces. Non-essential airframe stencilling was removed and pastel shades of blue and red formed the roundel colours.

Sea Harrier colours

The Sea Harriers suffered no losses in combat with Argentine Mirages and Skyhawks, but aircrew comments about the varied grey schemes used during the war centred on the fact that the best scheme for future use would be a compromise between the Extra Dark Sea Grey and the Medium Sea Grey. Lighter shades than these would certainly compromise aircraft flying over the sea when viewed from above, as Argentinian Navy Skyhawk pilots found to their costs — Light Gull Grey was their usual scheme — and since the war the Sea Harrier force has standardised on an overall satin or semi-gloss Dark Sea Grey colour which may not meet all the pilot's requirements but is probably an acceptable scheme for peacetime flying.

Biggest of all the naval air forces currently in existence is that of the United States, with over 1,800 combat aircraft in service. By tradition,

the US Navy and Marine Corps have consistently maintained highly decorated aircraft, units often vying with each other to produce the brightest and most flamboyant style of tail and fuselage insignia. Basic airframe colours (it would be a misnomer to call it camouflage) have been centred around the liberal use of gloss Light Gull Grey (FS 16440) over most surfaces although gloss white was a standard undersurface colour for many years on US Navy aircraft.

In 1981, however, the USN adopted and began implementing new toned-down camouflage schemes for its front-line fleet similar to those used by the USAF. The F-14 Tomcat, as the Navy's main interceptor, was given an official scheme of dark grey-blue (FS 35237) over the top surfaces, a medium grey (FS 36320) on the side of the fuselage and fins, and light grey (FS 36375) on the undersurfaces, while a similar arrangement is applied to the F-4J Phantoms and A-7E Corsairs. Markings have had the bright colours deleted and national insignia is in outline only. Deterioration is one of

US Navy F/A-18 Hornet

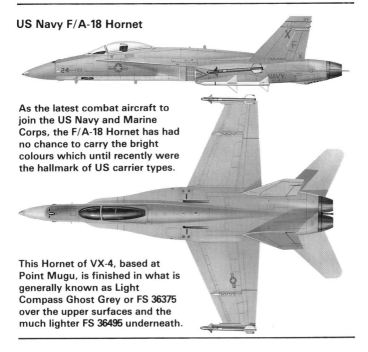

As the latest combat aircraft to join the US Navy and Marine Corps, the F/A-18 Hornet has had no chance to carry the bright colours which until recently were the hallmark of US carrier types.

This Hornet of VX-4, based at Point Mugu, is finished in what is generally known as Light Compass Ghost Grey or FS 36375 over the upper surfaces and the much lighter FS 36495 underneath.

the biggest problems of these matt or lustreless colours and such is the exposure of these schemes to the elements that it is often difficult to determine where the colours change. To prevent unnecessary scuffing of the surfaces maintenance crews are encouraged to wear protective footwear.

Although possessing no carriers, the West German Bundesmarine provides NATO with an extra combat force, its Tornado strike and Atlantic patrol aircraft being assigned to cover the Baltic and its environs. Standard Bundesmarine colours for these two aircraft and the Sea King and Lynx helicopters in use are Basalt Grey (RAL7012) over the top surfaces and Light Grey (RAL7035) on the undersurfaces.

Below: A new disruptive camouflage pattern of light and dark greys on a German Navy Tornado of MFG-1.

Bundesmarine Tornado

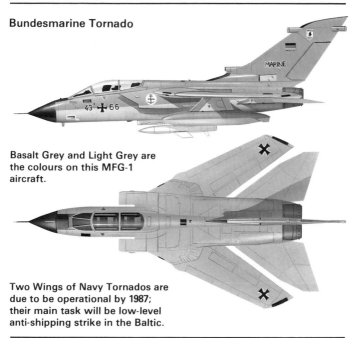

Basalt Grey and Light Grey are the colours on this MFG-1 aircraft.

Two Wings of Navy Tornados are due to be operational by 1987; their main task will be low-level anti-shipping strike in the Baltic.

On the Tornados the fuselage dividing line between the two colours runs along the mid-point, but the high visibility at distance of such a light surface has prompted trials with a random disruptive scheme of multiple-shade greys. Known as the Alberich scheme, this proposal has recently been accepted and will be progressively applied to the fleet. Hand-in-hand with this scheme is the general toning down of colour over the airframe, most markings being applied in black only.

The French Navy has two carriers in service, *Clemenceau* and *Foch*, and from these and its shore bases the Aéronavale operates a number of fixed-wing aircraft and helicopters. The premier combat type is the Dassault-Breguet Super Etendard, 71 having been procured by the Service for the strike-attack role. These were delivered in blue-grey and light grey colours, but ex-

Above: Two Spanish Navy AV-8A Matadors. No 3 appears to have a replacement rudder.

perience in brief operations over the Lebanon in 1983-84 revealed the need for a more effective camouflage for both overland and maritime flying. The result is the application of a disruptive pattern of two greys over the top surface, the lighter shade extending over the undersurfaces.

The Soviet Navy has four aircraft carriers, each equipped with a complement of Yak-38 V/STOL fighters and Kamov Ka-25 and Ka-27 helicopters. Painted blue-grey, the Yak-38s have shown no changes to the standard colour scheme since they were first deployed but it would be surprising if, when the next fixed-wing combat aircraft joins the Navy's new large carrier, the type eventually decided upon did not appear in a different colour.

Soviet Yak-38 'Forger'

The Yak-38 'Forger', the Soviet Navy's only fixed-wing carrier-based combat aircraft, operates from Kiev class ships.

All the Forgers in service have the same basic dark blue-grey colour scheme.

Special colours

Just as nature provides certain creatures with particular colours for protection and concealment from their enemies, so too do the camouflage specialists devise occasional one-off paint schemes for aircraft with special tasks. Sometimes, too, officialdom takes a back seat and units will decide themselves that in order to survive in a particular environment they need their machines finished in a certain way. Usually this originates with personal experience on the part of aircrew who might have survived being bounced by 'enemy' forces during exercises due to flying an aircraft painted in a totally unsuitable colour.

Snow schemes

One example is the finish applied to RAF Harriers and Jaguars, which form part of the UK's commitment to the defence of Northern Norway, during the winter period when a number of NATO exercises are held. The Harriers of 1 Sqn started it with a random coat of whitewash over the top surfaces, leaving the basic dark green-grey camouflage showing through to help break up the outline. Later, 41 Sqn went one better and devised a light blue and white scheme, again using a washable distemper, for their Jaguars. More recently the Jaguars have received large patches of white over their dark green-grey, reminiscent of the random schemes applied to Luftwaffe Bf 109s and He 111 bombers operating in this area during the 1939-45 war. One drawback with this temporary colouring is the appalling finish which results from a few days' intensive operations, but this is deemed a small penalty to pay when the camouflage is instrumental in enabling the aircraft to successfully complete their missions.

Below: An experimental winter scheme of white applied over the basic green/grey colours of a Jaguar of 41 Sqn, RAF, makes it almost invisible against a Norwegian mountainside.

What do you do when an aircraft the size of a four-jet Nimrod requires a new camouflage scheme? Such a question was posed to camouflage specialist Philip Barley at RAE Farnborough in the mid-1970s. Since the introduction of the Nimrod maritime patrol aircraft, it had operated in a finish of gloss white on top and light grey underneath, and its Achilles heel was the glint which continually bounced off the curved surface of the fuselage and from the cockpit area. A flat surface will normally only glint instantaneously — enough to attract attention but without necessarily continuing to show — but a sustained glint will give the game away completely. A toning down was required, and as the big aircraft spent a considerable time on the ground at open air dispersals, a colour was needed that would closely match concrete.

Concrete camouflage

As a result of colour and reflectance research, Hemp was chosen as the shade that matched concrete most closely, and when an aircraft was painted and flown in comparative trials with a white Nimrod it was found that in almost all air-to-air situations it was better than the old scheme — an example of a scheme geared to an airfield background pro-

Above: With the main intention of camouflaging aircraft against large areas of concrete hardstandings, the RAF's Nimrod MR.2 maritime patrol force was given a scheme of Hemp over the top surfaces and Light Grey underneath. Although the machines on the ground are clearly visible in this view, a potential high speed, low-level attacker could have problems.

ving just as good if not better in the air. So the Nimrod force has been steadily receiving the Hemp and grey camouflage as each aircraft comes up for major servicing, and the RAF has also specified the scheme for the VC10 tanker fleet.

Colour confusion

Sometimes colour schemes go wrong, not just on a single aircraft such as the first Hemp-coloured Nimrod which was finished in dark brown and subsequently had to be repainted, but en masse, as illustrated by the 15 ex-US Navy F-4J Phantoms acquired by the RAF to maintain the strength of UK-based air defences following the deployment of 23 Sqn to the Falklands in 1982. When the re-worked F-4J(UK) Phantoms arrived at their Wattisham base for 74 Sqn, their colours were

Above: An example of how two different air forces tackle the same problem. In the foreground, a USAF KC-10 Extender air refuelling tanker finished in the charcoal colour which has become the standard camouflage for this type of aircraft. On the right is an RAF VC10 tanker which has the Hemp and Light Grey scheme. The Hemp shade approximates to BS2660-4-049.

Below: The black finish over all but the upper surfaces of this MC-130E Hercules of the 7th Special Operations Squadron, USAF, serves two purposes: first to absorb radar signals and second to reduce visual acquisition during the highly classified missions undertaken by this unit. The 7th is based in Germany; other units are based in Florida and the Philippines.

Above: If you can't conceal it —
confuse it! This F-16XL prototype
was given a shaded diagonal
scheme with a false fin shadow,
cockpit and refuelling marking on
the underside.

Below: Known as rectilinear
disruptive camouflage, this
scheme was devised by artist
Keith Ferris and tested by the US
Navy on six F-14A Tomcats
during trials in 1977.

USAF Aggressor F-5E

This F-5E Aggressor aircraft is based at RAF Alconbury, UK, and wears the scheme known as 'Frog'. Note the latest stencilled national insignia and USAF on the wings.

The disruptive schemes applied to Aggressor aircraft are intended to depict colour combinations used by Eastern Bloc air arms, adding realism to training.

noticeably different from those on 56 Sqn FGR.2s. The scheme should have conformed with the standard Phantom colours (Light Aircraft Grey/Medium Sea Grey/Barley Grey) but the semi-matt finish was applied by the US Navy using American colours — Neutral Grey (FS 36170), Barley Grey equivalent (FS 36314) and Gull Grey (FS 36440). The high quality finish was found to be much easier to keep clean than the UK matt finish, but it is expected that the aircraft will revert to the standard colours when individual machines are sent to RAF St Athan for routine maintenance.

Aggressor schemes

To increase and maintain the fighting skills of front-line pilots, the USAF and US Navy operate a number of Aggressor combat training squadrons. Equipped with Northrop F-5Es and two-seat F-5Fs, types with similar performances to that of the MiG-21, these units take realism very seriously, to the extent that they decorate their crew rooms with Soviet flags, posters and pictures; more importantly, their aircraft carry camouflage schemes representative of the colours used by Warsaw Pact

Above: Hardly camouflage, but typical of the gaudy markings often applied for special occasions. This Belgian F-16A was the star attraction at the 1985 NATO Tiger Meet. Specially coloured latex was used, applied over seven coats of primer to protect the aircraft's anti-radar paint. Only one flight was made in these colours as it was found that large areas peeled in the air.

Below: Three anniversaries in one. The RAF painted this F-4 Phantom in 1979 to mark the 60th anniversary of the crossing of the Atlantic by Alcock and Brown in 1919 and also included the 30th anniversary of NATO and Rolls-Royce's 60 years of aero engine production at Derby. It landed at Greenham Common on June 21, having crossed the Atlantic in just over five hours.

and other Eastern air forces. The multi-coloured schemes have unofficial names such as 'grey ghost', 'patches', 'frog' and 'snake'. Colours vary widely from greens and greys to blues and browns, some machines having a markedly dark appearance while others are much lighter. As new information becomes available to the units, so the colours are changed to maintain up-to-the-minute appearances for the crews exercising against the Aggressors. Large two-digit numbers are painted on the noses of the F-5s, usually the last two of the serial number, outlined in the style of Soviet Bort numbers.

Although camouflage is used to conceal, it can also be used to deceive. American artist Keith Ferris has developed a number of extreme colour schemes intended to confuse enemy pilots as to the exact attitude of the aircraft, including the hard-edged zig-zag patterns in blues and greys trialled by the USAF and USN, but complete adoption of this type of colouring has yet to be made.

One style was tried on the F-16XL cranked-arrow delta wing dual-role fighter nick-named The Wedge. The second of the two prototypes built was given a deceptive diagonally

striped top-surface scheme of Neutral Grey, Light Ghost Grey, Intermediate Grey and Gunship Grey. This was continued on the under-surface and the layout, devised by Lt Cdr Heatley (USN), became known as the Heatley-Ferris Scheme. It was found that the colours deceived without compromising detection, but performed better against dark backgrounds. The aircraft was given a false painted canopy under the nose plus a false vertical tail and shadow, in-flight refuelling marks and outline national insignia on the fuselage to form a mirror image of the top surface, though the ultimate step of painting missiles with false shadows and an engine intake on the top surface was not taken.

Show schemes
Some colours painted on combat aircraft have the totally opposite effect of concealing them. The annual Tiger Meet held by NATO squadrons with a Tiger in their badge has regularly encouraged flamboyant colour schemes. Black and yellow stripes have been painted on a number of different aircraft types including Starfighters, F-16s, Phantoms and even a Puma helicopter, often accompanied by a large tiger's head on the nose. The application of these schemes and others which celebrate anniversaries of units or famous personnel is not always encouraged by officialdom: painting complicated designs on an aircraft can be very time-consuming, and some unit commanders would argue that it also impairs squadron efficiency. An acceptable compromise is often worked out however, such as a coloured tail or a particularly graphic piece of nose art.

With all the research and experimentation expended on finding the correct camouflage for today's modern warplane, perhaps it is sobering to reflect that nature has already sorted out the problem. Birds have colours suitable for their environment and in a sense they have the same fundamental problem — to catch their prey without being seen. Maybe the camouflage experts should take a leaf out of their book — or maybe they already have.

OTHER SUPER-VALUE MILITARY GUIDES IN THIS SERIES......

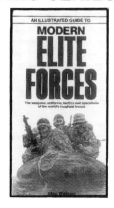

Air War over Vietnam
Allied Fighters of World War II
Battleships and Battlecruisers
Bombers of World War II
German, Italian and Japanese Fighters
  of World War II
Israeli Air Force
Military Helicopters
Modern Airborne Missiles
Modern Destroyers
Modern Fighters and Attack Aircraft
Modern Soviet Air Force
Modern Soviet Ground Forces

Modern Soviet Navy
Modern Sub Hunters
Modern Submarines
Modern Tanks
Modern US Air Force
Modern US Army
Modern US Navy
Modern Warships
NATO Fighters
Pistols and Revolvers
Rifles and Sub-machine Guns
Space Warfare
World War II Tanks

✱ Each has 160 fact-filled pages
✱ Each is colourfully illustrated with hundreds of action photos and technical drawings
✱ Each contains concisely presented data and accurate descriptions of major international weapons
✱ Each represents tremendous value

If you would like further information on any of our titles please write to:
Publicity Dept. (Military Div.), Salamander Books Ltd.,
52 Bedford Row, London WC1R 4LR